"IT'S THE FOLLOW-UP, STUPID!"

A REVOLUTIONARY COVERT SELLING FORMULA TO DOUBLING YOUR BUSINESS AT ZERO COST THANKS TO AUTOMATED EMAIL CAMPAIGNS

TIZ GAMBACORTA

CONTENTS

ACKNOWLEDGEMENTS

I would like to thank my partner Claire Morgan for her invaluable input in making what started as an idea whilst we were trekking in Nepal, a reality. Without her, this book would never have seen the light of day.

I would also like to thank:

- Mark Anastasi, for initially educating me to digital marketing through his seminars and more recently, helping shape the original concept for this book.

- Ryan Hamada, for also physically taking me to some of Mark's seminars and making the three-year long business-building journey with me. More recently, I would also like to thank him for providing feedback on some parts of the contents behind and around this book.

- Antonio Moreno Lewis for providing invaluable "hands on" marketing feedback on the production of this book.

I would also like to thank the following people who knowingly or unknowingly, consciously or unconsciously, contributed to the contents of this book through their wisdom and through some of our conversations: Shawn Janji, Hadar Swersky, Maor Lahav, Kip Gienau, Ryan Deiss and Richard Lindner.

I would also like to thank my former manager at Barclays Capital in London, UK Nicolas Tjandramaga. Most people would consider having to report to a manager as one of the frustrations and lowlights of their careers. However, thanks to Nic's financial derivatives and management genius, reporting to him was actually one of my highlights of employed life. Whilst after my 9-year career as an investment banker and derivatives trader I eventually discovered that employee life was not for me, I will always remember our (very) unpolitically-correct sense of humour both on the desk and during our business travels. Needless to say, this didn't make either of us conform to the "typical" stereotype of the polished, pin-striped British banker

I would also like to thank several editors and proofreaders who helped making the contents clearer and eliminate many of the errors. Sometimes you will notice grammar and punctuation will have been bent in favour of driving a point home. In the context of clarity, persuasion and helping the reader achieve results, schoolbook grammar holds no bearing at all. As one of my mentors Dan Kennedy likes to say "There is a reason why teachers get paid like they do and successful entrepreneurs get paid like they do". If you are in the academic profession, take no offence. Having said this, I take full responsibility for any errors or omissions. If you spot any, please email me directly on t@dvfx.com.

If you enjoyed this book, don't forget to leave a review here: http://amzn.com/B01CH5MM06. We may be selecting some reviewers at random with surprise gifts to say 'thank you'.

INTRODUCTION

Where You're Missing Out On Millions Of Dollars

Since the late 2000, a revolution has taken place in the way people do business. Thanks to drag and drop web-based software, you can now automate your email marketing *without any technical or marketing background*.

Tens of thousands of small, medium and large businesses are marketing to their customers (including you) thanks to automated software that does all the work for them- literally whilst they sleep. After all, if billions have been invested in marketing automation tools that are available for just a few dollars a month, would you want to take advantage of this opportunity to double your business hands-free?

This revolution is gathering momentum. Forrester Research estimates that $327 billion will be spent online in 2016. According to the marketing analytics platform Monetate, email marketing drives more conversions than any other marketing channel, including search and social. 92% of online adults use email, with 61% using it on an average day. Those who were most likely to use email on a daily basis were those with a college degree or an income of more than $75,000. And yet, most businesses are completely unaware of the opportunity that automated email marketing has created for them and their future wealth.

This book and its related blog share the success stories of 100s of businesses and students of mine. Including...

- How Michelle Dale took her three kids on a ten year holiday around the world and makes $30,000 a month by keeping in touch with her email list

- How 62-year old Joel Friendlander made $10,000 in a few days during his first product launch to his 1,400 strong list

- How Dana Levy started a mailing list from (literally) nothing in 2000 and sold it in 2008 for $125 million

- How Milk&More is getting 1 in 5 of its prospects and inactive customers to order again through triggered emails

- How Morgan Brown is making $4,000/month thanks to automated email sequences

- How British insurer Liverpool Victoria is making £198.40 for every £1 it spends thanks to behaviour-based email marketing

- How electric bike manufacturer Jim Turner, grew sales from $532,000 to $1.45million, increased leads by 83% and added an extra 10 holidays per year by automating his sales funnel

- How photographer Tyler Smith reduced staff by two, grew revenue 21% in the first year and increased leads from 200 to 19,576 thanks to automated appointment scheduling

- How Debbie Green in California, USA increased sales by 38% by automating her email follow up

- How wedding enthusiast Julie Goldman in NJ, USA grew sales by 60% by automating how her clients requested quotes

- How Oxford-educated Joanna Penn went on to become a New York Times and USA Today best-selling author and built a $100,000+/year book publishing and coaching business by keeping in regular contact with her email list

- How Fran Kerr is making $4,000-$12,000/month in income by publishing eBooks and selling them to her email list

- How German energy giant RWE exceeded its target by 267% by sending automated, behaviour-based emails to its customers

- How health spa entrepreneur Joe Stone in California, USA doubled his sales in one year thanks to automated email follow ups

- How internet giant Amazon.com increased sales by $300 million/year by running an A/B test on a single button!

- How Heather Lemere from Salon Success Strategies in California, USA increased yearly revenue by 300%, reduced costs by 40%, and rarely works more than 8 hours/day thanks to automated lead nurturing

- How Meny Hoffman and his marketing agency in Tennessee, USA reduced ad spend by 24%, grew customers by 15% and boosted revenue by over $1 million thanks to a Welcome Program, a Selling Campaign and direct mail (these will be covered in detail later in the book)

- How Missouri, USA dentist Dr. Burleson is converting 85% of his leads into patients thanks to automated email follow up. As a result, revenues grew 180%, acquisition costs reduced by 56% and his yearly vacation days went from 5 to 42!

- How coach Tom Menditto uses his email list to made $30,000/month within 12 months by helping others overcome ADHD

- How online retailer Paper Style increased email open rates by 244%, increased click through rates by 161%,and grew revenue per mailing by 330% thanks to action-based grouping in less than 8 weeks

- How ecommerce shop Fabric.com increased conversions by more than 50% thanks to automated email campaigns based around birthdays, anniversaries, etc.

- How Olivier Roland started making €14,000/month teaching fellow French nationals how to start a business after emailing his list of 300 subscribers

- How retail chain Moosejaw increased conversion rates by 461% thanks to email list segmentation

- How Jim Cavale, Forrest Walden and their company Iron Tribe Fitness increased leads by 308%, profits by 310% and sold 60 franchises across the USA since 2012

- How software reseller Bridgevine increased conversions by 300% when they automated their email and SMS campaigns

- How animal welfare charity RSPCA achieved a 780% ROI from campaign segmentation and testing

In this book I also share with you how I met my mentor - and how his teaching helped me to go from a miserable job in my 20's to selling millions of dollars worth of products online.

You will discover in these pages...

- How I went from $20 to $5,000 a month in 8 weeks thanks to list building

- How I went from $5,000 to $50,000 a month thanks to email marketing automation

- How I turned $11.50 into $138,000 thanks to list segmentation

- How I went (again) from $0 to $52,000 a month thanks to "Selling Without Selling"

- And many more strategies that I've never revealed before now.

I am not mentioning these numbers to impress you. As a matter of fact, others are making much more money than I am. Instead, I am simply illustrating the fact that email marketing and marketing automation really works and can help you generate sales whilst you sleep (literally!). Small and large businesses alike are making fortunes online thanks to the marketing automation revolution.

You can now compete on a level-playing field with giants like Amazon thanks to advanced marketing automation software that, up to just a few years ago, was only available to those with budgets in the 8 or 9 figures range.

So, if you are stuck in your business because you are not able to get enough leads, convert enough customers or simply working too many hours this book will show you how you can generate more leads, more revenue and reduce your workload thanks to email marketing automation.

If you don't have a business, even better!

This book will show you some of the best practices to get started and will help you avoid the common mistakes that cause 95% of new businesses to fail.

If I could, I would reach out to you and grab you, shake you and scream at the top of my lungs: *"Wake up! You don't have to spend long days in the office just to make a living! Let email marketing automation do the lead generation and the selling so you don't have to do it! Just do it!"*

SECTION 1

WHAT'S IN IT FOR YOU?

1. The Single Biggest Opportunity You May Ever Face In Your Lifetime

This is the critical moment where you, as the business owner, have the choice to be squashed under the heel of the growing giant we know as artificial intelligence, or take up arms and ride into battle alongside a would-be-enemy, turning it into your greatest ally.

Back in 1995 the majority of people hadn't even heard of the internet, let alone email. Now, as we enter 2016, probably 90% of businesses out there have websites and of that 90% a growing number are realizing, "wait a minute, there's more to this internet thing that just having a website. Other people are out there using this "email thing" and not to just reach out to friends and family but also to grow their business. I want to do the same! How do I do that?"

I predict that in the next three years we're going to see almost 100% of businesses use email advertising in some way, shape or form. It will be similar to five years ago, when business owners accepted a website as being a necessity for their companies. As a matter of fact the number of business emails sent in 2015 went up 9% compared to 2014 and that percentage is expected to increase by 21% over the next three years.

This shift in consciousness represents the single biggest opportunity we may ever face in our lifetime. And the people who understand and grab this opportunity will make fortunes. I believe that we, as business leaders, are in the perfect position to make the most of this fundamental shift.

Email is the first thing that 58% of users check in the morning. In fact, email is the most regular part of online activities for 94% of users. If that wasn't enough, 77% of users prefer to receive commercial communication by email rather than other avenues such as phones and social media. There are billions of emails being sent out every day, and your prospects and your clients are being marketed to in very smart ways by your competitors (and sometimes not so smart ways, too).

Businesses that understand and seize this opportunity will prosper when using the tools that we have available to us correctly - and if you don't have the tools just yet, get them together as soon as possible. This is a hugely unique opportunity, and we as business leaders, can improve the quality of service we give, reducing our costs and leaving a legacy behind for those we love- all at the same time. If you want to do these things and more, then you should realize by now that automated email follow up is a must for your business. You can double your business thanks to automated email follow up and artificial intelligence. Befriend the giant, and he will become your greatest ally.

How Mother of Three Michelle Dale Takes Her Kids Around Europe on a Ten Year "Laptop Lifestyle" Trip To The Tune Of $30,000 A Month Thanks To Her Email List

As a former mortgage advisor in the UK, Michelle Dale quit her job in 2005 after she decided she wanted to leave the country and start traveling. As she needed to fund the travelling she figured out it would have to be through some sort of online business. She started working as a freelance virtual assistant for clients. Over time other people started asking her for help on how to virtual assistants.

In 2010 she decided to create an online training course showing others how they too could become virtual assistants and travel the world like she did. By then she had gathered a small list of 500 made up of friends and family and decided to email them announcing she would be releasing a training program. She sent a follow up email and ran a competition for a handful of beta-testing slots. The beta-testers would be given free access to the program in exchange for providing early feedback and helping it to improve. Out of the 41 people who applied, Michelle chose 7 beta testers.

She then sent an email to the 34 people who applied but didn't get the free beta-tester copy saying "I'm sorry you didn't win the free competition, but if you want to join us, it's $997 for the program." 19 people purchased, yielding **$18,943** in revenue in just a few weeks' time from promoting to a list of just 500 people!

"All right, what can I do better, what can I do more of?", thought Michelle. Thanks to her email list, she now has 6 online courses and averages **$27,000 to $30,000** every time she launches a new product to her list!

Find out more about Michelle Dales' story here:
http://ItsTheFollowupStupid.com/michelledale

How A 62 Year-Old Made $10,000 In Income From His Very First Launch To A 1,400 List!

Joel Friedlander started as a service provider to the publishing industry helping authors get published back in the 1980s before the self-publishing revolution. As the mortgage crisis hit, Joel started a blog in 2009. The blog started getting more and more popular but it wasn't generating much revenue. "Early 2012, I really started aggressively trying to build my email list which I had pretty much neglected before then.", says Joel. Shortly after thanks to a lead magnet, he was adding 1,000 subscribers per month to his mailing list.

He put together a training program for people who wanted to learn how to get into book publishing called "The Self-Publishing Roadmap". "I launched it off my email list and the first time I launched it, I had 1,400 people on my email list, which is not a very big list. It generated almost **$10,000** in income on that very first launch.

I realized that email was the way that was going to make this all work for me. And, that's how I work now. I use the blog as a platform and traffic generation and all my business and sales are done through email promotions, whether they're my own products or somebody else's.", says Joel.

After that, thanks to email marketing and Jeff Walker's Product Launch Formula Joel has run email campaigns that have made from $33,000 to $46,000 in just five days. Need we say more?

Find out more about Joel's story here:
http://ItsTheFollowupStupid.com/joelfriedlander

2. The Four-Word Magic Principle That Doubled My Business

Who ever graduated out of university thinking, "I want to become an email marketer!"? Not many people I guess. The idea for this book came into being several years ago after attending a marketing seminar in London, UK. One of these speakers said something quite poignant; something that would echo in my head for years to come. He said,

> *"Guys, if you have a business, you know this. Statistically speaking, 81% of sales come after 5 or more contacts. But 85% of the time, business owners or sales people stop after just 1 or 2 contacts.* **It's the follow-up, stupid***!"*

I saw the value in this concept and realized that it was an idea that needed to be shared with other business owners. I decided to write a book about email marketing automation because it has revolutionized the way I do business! Many consider me a voice of authority in the online marketing industry and I have personally identified and implemented each of the steps and strategies discussed later in this book.

The adept reader may also have noticed that the title of this book was derived from James Carville's famous incitement to Bill Clinton's 1992 campaign staff called "*It's the Economy, Stupid!*" It's a bit of a play on words, because much of what you will learn in this book will probably have you thinking, "Duh! That's what I should have been focusing on!"

This book was written in an effort to bring this revolutionary marketing approach to business owners around the globe. The series of steps listed in this book are important elements to the success of my achievements in business. Though you may come from a very different background to mine, the goal of this book will apply to all: to help you and your business reach its fullest potential.

I first decided to write 'It's the Follow-Up, Stupid!' after noticing that many businesses were spending unnecessary time and resources in futile attempts to acquire clientele. These businesses were paying a lot more money to connect with and educate their customer base, and yet their results were minute at best. I knew that connecting with and educating clients could be done easily and automatically at a much lower cost. I knew that marketing automation was the future key to success for the modern entrepreneur.

My introduction to the world of email marketing took place in 2010 at a seminar that renowned digital marketer, Mark Anastasi, happened to speak at. I remember him distinctly saying "Email marketing is the only way to sell to your prospects and clients over and over again, automatically, without having to spend any more money on lead generation". It suddenly dawned on me how emailing your list equals power - a very strange kind of power. But we'll talk about this special kind of power later.

I learned that email marketing and list building presented a whole new form of strength and possibilities to business owners. I began to put together a list of prospects, and as the business grew with time, (ranging from $36,000 to $50,000 a month), I recognized that I'd run into a slight problem. As my responsibilities grew along with the business, it suddenly became a gruelling and impossible task for me to follow up with such a large, expanding customer base in a streamlined and effective way.

This was a critical moment for me in my career and, recognizing it as an opportunity rather than a moment of despair, I began investing much of my time and effort into the art of automatic follow-up. This became the crux of my belief in the personalization of marketing automation.

3. Marketing Automation: Can You Really Make More By Working Less?

Simply put, marketing automation is the ability to send out targeted marketing messages to your prospect and clients without having to manually send out those messages. Your marketing message is sent out to each of your prospects or clients based on triggers – when they joined your mailing list, when they buy a product, when it's their birthday, when they visit your website, when they don't complete an order form, and so on.

If you have or are thinking about having a business, you have or will have a large database of prospects and customers. They all have different wants, needs and expectations from you. They all have different education levels, different spending habits and an overall mix of varying lifestyles. How will you connect with them - ALL of them - quickly and easily?

The answer is *analyzing user behaviour*. There is power in the ability to tap into a database and pinpoint a customer's likes and dislikes, all in a matter of seconds. By analyzing behaviour and the type of content each customer responds to, marketing automation systems have the ability to track and automate emails and marketing material based on each individual's preference. This allows for personalization on an automated level, and gives us a chance to automate targeted communications with our customer base on a large scale.

How Bridgevine Increased Conversion Rates By 300% Thanks To A Selling Campaign

Bridgevine, a reseller of cable and telecommunications, was facing the challenge that the majority of their prospects were not calling into the company call centre to set up their installations and, therefore, they were not becoming clients.

In an effort to be more proactive rather than merely reactive, to their prospective clients, Bridgevine implemented an automated email and SMS campaign whereby anyone who filled in their details on the company website and did not immediately schedule an appointment for installation would be entered into a Selling Campaign (we will cover this in detail later in the book).

During this campaign Bridgevine would send the prospect a series of automated SMS and emails for the 3 days following the submission of the form on the website.

"This powerful capability enables us to give our prospects real-time messages that result in **immediate ROI for our business**. We are excited to expand our SMS and email programs to **provide true one-to-one relationships** with more of our prospects", says Adam Berlin, Marketing Manager.

By triggering messages to their prospects based on their behaviour Bridgevine was able to **increase their conversion rate by 300%**, with a call-back rate of 33%.

Find out more about Bridgevine's story here:
http://ItsTheFollowupStupid.com/bridgevine

The technology used for marketing automation these days can offer a host of insights to help you grow your business and revenues thanks to the data it provides. It allows you to identify the 20% of your customers who are clicking on more links in your emails and buying the most products from you. These are the 20% of people who are responsible for 80% or more of your sales.

Knowing who makes up this all-important, revenue generating 20% means that you can focus the majority of your energy on them and stop spending too much time on the 80% of people who only give you 20% of your sales. After Italian economist Pareto initially coming up with the concept, Perry Marshall in his book *80/20 Sales and Marketing* demonstrated extensively how there is no business where this 80/20 rule doesn't apply in one way or the other.

How Iron Tribe Fitness Boosted Net Profits by 310% With Pre-Built Email Templates

In just a few short years, Iron Tribe Fitness went from a garage gym for friends to 6 fitness centre locations and 60 franchisees across the south-eastern USA.

Co-Owner, Forrest Waldon, states, "We have several different tags and actions that occur, depending on the information entered within each web form. We have two different free reports [lead magnets] written with classic direct response elements including bold headlines, an irresistible offer, ironclad guarantees and social proof. Another standard action is a 12-step follow-up email sequence that educates the prospect on the nine fundamental movements of our Iron Tribe program."

Being able to identify and tag leads coming into the business depending on what form was filled in has allowed iron Tribe fitness to effectively and automatically use pre-built email templates to close the sale – seeing their **net profits increase by 310%**.

Find out more about Iron Tribe's story here:
http://ItsTheFollowupStupid.com/irontribefitness

4. Email And Grow Rich

Email marketing is communicating to your prospect or customer through email. However, it is not the mid-90's anymore and today's buyer has an upper hand when it comes to purchasing decisions. Tech savvy and sophisticated, they are wise to the ways of email marketing and can spot a sale email from miles away. Gone are the days when an email was the cause of excitement – now, they have high expectations and demands when it comes to the emails they choose to open and consume. They believe you should inform and entertain, but never bore or, worse, irritate. And they're fickle when it comes to email messages - if you don't keep communications interesting, they are likely to opt-out from your list and will have no problems with marking you as "spam" if you fail to meet expectations.

How Dana Levy Went From $0 to $125 Million in 8 Years

Dana started her Daily Candy email list by emailing friends and family until she grew it to 700 people strong. Building this initial list cost her *nothing*. Her email newsletter catered to the 24 to 35 year old city woman who loves shopping and being in the know.

She started working on the email marketing business in January 2011 and went live in March that same year. Within a year by leveraging technology, Daily Candy's newsletter was turning a profit. Two years later Levy was wooed by the Pilot Group at which point she sold a controlling stake to venture capitalist Bob Pittman for $3.5 million. And in 2008 Daily Candy was sold to Comcast for a healthy *$125 million* but since Levy also retained a 20% interest in the business, that meant she walked away from the sale with a cool $25 million. Not bad after having started from 0!

Find out more about Dana's story here:
http://ItsTheFollowupStupid.com/danalevy

The French Blogger Who Makes 14,000 EUR a Month With An Email List Of Just 300 Subscribers!

Olivier Roland began as an entrepreneur running a computer software and hardware company when he was just 19, but soon found that the 70 hour weeks he was working wasn't giving him the lifestyle he desired. He moved on to world of blogging for French audiences and gathered a list of 300 email subscribers.

He then surveyed his audience asking them "what is the greatest frustration or problem you currently face?" The answer was procrastination and a lack of success launching their own business. Having had his own business for ten years, Olivier knew he could teach in this area and decided to launch a training program on how to start a business.

After the launch he had a €3,000 a month income stream, charging €47/month for the standard training program and €97/month for the premium version. Three months later, after networking with various French bloggers and recruiting some of them as affiliates, he did a full public launch taking his monthly income to €14,000/ month.

Find out more about Olivier's story here:
http://ItsTheFollowupStupid.com/olivierroland

5. 12 Reasons Why You Must Use Email Marketing In Your Business

Reason 1: Email Marketing Allows You To Control Your Audience

When you have a large following on Facebook, Twitter or Google, for example, the social platform or company own those names; you do not. They can shut down your account anytime, without any warning. When you have a mailing list, you own and control that audience.

Reason 2: Email Marketing Allows You To Leverage Technology In A Massive Scale

Think about this for a minute. If you have 10,000 subscribers on your mailing list you can communicate anytime with 10,000 prospects and customer*s at zero cost*!

It's almost like being able to do business with 10,000 people instantly, over and over again.

Reason 3: Email Marketing Allows You To Do Business Anywhere In The World

Thanks to email marketing you can communicate with your prospects and customers, regardless of where they are in the world and you can do that from anywhere in the world.

Reason 4: Email Marketing Allows You To Do Business Anytime

In the same way that you can communicate with your prospects and client <u>from</u> anywhere in the world, <u>to</u> anywhere in the world, you can also do business with them regardless of time zones.

Email marketing allows you to communicate with all of your prospects no matter what time you send your email or what time it is received.

Reason 5: Email Marketing Allows You To Communicate With Your Entire Audience Instantly

If you have 10,000 subscribers on your list and there is a specific announcement in the market you want to share with them, you can let everyone know at the same time, *instantly*.

Likewise, if you are launching a new product, they will all be able to buy from you the moment it's available. No more having to call people individually, call again if they're unavailable, send letters in the post, publish press releases etc. You can communicate with your entire audience directly and as the saying goes, "the early bird catches the worm".

Reason 6: Email Marketing Allows You To Personalize Your Messages

Most traditional forms of marketing, such as television, newspaper advertising and direct mail, require a "one-size-fits-all" format, meaning that it's difficult for you to speak directly to your consumer in a personalized way.

With email marketing on the other hand, not only can you send a personalized email with your user's name or login name, but you can also feed in personalized information such as sales or purchase history. For example, you can select all of your prospects or customers who are in San Francisco and then write your message to speak directly about San Francisco.

With email marketing you can easily speak to your customers in a very personalized and intimate way that is not possible with other marketing channels.

Reason 7: Email Marketing Allows You To Target Your Messages

Because you can segment your database of prospects and customers, you can send extremely targeted marketing campaigns that will result in increased sales conversions *simply because they are so specific*. For example, if you sell flowers, you can find everybody in your database who ever bought daffodils and then send them an email in April when the first daffodil shipments come in. You're then using email marketing to put the most relevant message in front of the customers who are most likely to respond to it. That's what good marketing is all about.

Reason 8: More Frequent Communication

Because email takes less time to create and send, and is less costly than other marketing and advertising channels, you can communicate with your audience more frequently.

Instead of only being able to send them a flyer or catalogue once a month or once a quarter, you can easily send them offers once a week, or even daily.

Reason 9: Test Marketing Messages

With email marketing, it becomes incredibly easy to see what graphics, headlines, offers and even colours your users and customers respond to. You can see how many people opened an email, how many people clicked a link in an email, which specific link within the email was clicked, how many people unsubscribed and, of course, whether your email even made it into your recipient's inbox.

Through some of the email marketing automation tools discussed in this book, you can figure out which marketing message worked better to generate leads and sales... and then do it more.

Reason 10: Email Marketing Means You Can Give Yourself A Pay Raise Every Month

According to online marketing expert Ryan Deiss, pure digital businesses should be making on average $1 per subscriber per month. So if your business is 100% digital and you have a mailing list of 5,000 people you should be making $5,000 per month. If your list is 20,000 strong you should be making $20,000 per month and so on.

Direct marketer Andrew Reynolds takes this concept up one level: "For every 1,000 customers on your list (i.e. those who paid you a sum of money, no matter the amount), you should be averaging $157,335 in yearly sales from them".

US marketer John Alanis takes it one notch further up and states: "For every 1,000 customers on your list who have paid $300 or more, you can make $1,000,000 a year in sales from them".

Want to give yourself a pay raise and make an extra $1,000 per month? Just add 1,000 subscribers to your list!

Reason 11: People Who Are On Your Email List Will Buy A Lot More From You

From my own offers, a landing page may convert at 45% from email traffic whereas it will convert at 10% (at best) from cold traffic. Email traffic is someone who got to your website after receiving an email from you, while cold traffic is someone who got to your website by clicking on a banner for example. Likewise, 1 in 200 people may buy from you if they are from cold traffic versus 1 in 10 people buying from you if they are on your emailing list.

You can make 20x more money from your email list than you can from other sources. And that's not all. Once you paid for the cost of acquisition of that subscriber you can promote them with offers over and over at no additional cost. With other sources of traffic, if you want to promote more offers you have to buy that traffic all over again.

Last but not least, once you build an email list it becomes a sellable asset you can retail together or separately from your business (I have done this very successfully on websites like Flippa.com).

Reason 12: Save The Planet!

It may seem like a minor part of the big picture, but when you optimize email marketing as a primary communication channel, you'll help save the planet by reducing the number of trees killed for print marketing pieces.

Still Not Convinced?

- 95% of online consumers have an email account.

- The total number of worldwide email accounts is expected to increase to over 4.3 billion accounts by year-end 2016. (Radicati Group)

- 57% of email subscribers spend 10-60 minutes browsing marketing emails during the week. (ChoozOn)

- Knowledge workers on average spend 13 of their working hours each week in their email inbox. (McKinsey & Company)

- Email is 40x more successful at acquiring new clients than either Facebook and Twitter. (McKinsey & Company)

- 42% of B2B organizations say email is one of their most effective lead generators for targeting new clients. (Circle Research)

- When it comes to purchases made as a result of receiving a marketing message, email has the highest conversion rate (66%), when compared to social, direct mail and more. (Direct Marketing Association)

- One study showed that email is the second most used marketing tool (after a company website) for B2B companies. (eMarketer)

Email Marketing Vs. Social Media

- 22% emails will not reach the inbox. 74% of Facebook Fans will not even know you posted something. (MarketingProfs)

- 75% of the reach froma Facebook post happens in less than 2 hrs but an Email needs to be killed to reach its life-span. (WiseMetrics)

- 77% prefer email to receive promotional content, while only 4% prefer Facebook (MarketingLand)

- 78% of marketing emails are sent to a personal email account. (ChoozOn)

- There are 3x more email accounts than Twitter and Facebook accounts combined. (Radicati Group)

- You are 6x more likely to get a click-through from an email campaign than you are from a tweet. (Campaign Monitor)

Neil Patel: "Email Continually Outperforms"

"Out of all the channels I tested as a marketer, email continually outperforms most of them. Not only does it have a high conversion rate, but as you build up your list you can continually monetize it by pitching multiple products. Just look at ecommerce sites like Amazon, one way they get you to continually buy more products from them is by emailing you offers on a regular basis."

Neil Patel – Cofounder of KISSmetrics & Crazy Egg

Marketing Automation + Email Marketing = More Leads, More Sales

With email marketing automation, instead of you having to write these messages every time, automation helps you send the right marketing message to the right person at the right time in the right format.

Noah Kagan: "90%+ Of Our Revenue Comes From Automated Emails"

"Email is the most scalable way to make sales with new customers and build deeper relationship with deeper customers. AppSumo. com is a 7 figure business and 90%+ of our revenue comes from automated emails."

Noah Kagan – Founder of SumoMe

6. You + Marketing Automation = An Online ATM?

Today, thanks to marketing automation and email marketing, entrepreneurs are building million and billion-dollar businesses. They have the freedom to travel anytime they want, reduce their office headcount, hire anywhere in the world and work anytime they want. Why? Because marketing automation is doing most of the marketing and selling *for* them.

In his book, *Rich Dad, Poor Dad*, author Robert Kiyosaki explains that to escape what I call the "entrepreneurial rat race", you need to invest your time and resources in building income-producing assets (for example rental properties or business processes that generate income by themselves). The goal is eventually to have these assets run the business for you so that you're not needed anymore. That's how you achieve true business success.

When I started my online marketing in 2011 I had no knowledge, no assets, and no email list to promote anything to. To make things worse, I had an expensive London lifestyle to fund and a large mortgage to pay. Hiring staff wasn't an option because I didn't have the income to support the cost. Instead, I decided to leverage technology to serve as large an audience as possible. Eventually, leveraging this technology would go on to generate thousands of dollars a day.

By the time I reached my early 30s, I had 12,000 clients in 64 countries and 4 different income streams. I could work (or not work) from home or while travelling the world… because I had marketing automation running my businesses for me.

Imagine having a business that…

- Can cost practically nothing to setup

- Doesn't need staff to run

- Doesn't need offices

- You can run from home or anywhere in the world

- Markets to your customers automatically, 365 days a year, 24/7

- Has other people selling your products for you, *for free*! (e.g. affiliates)

- Runs on autopilot (people buy your products from your websites without human intervention)

- Allows you to leverage increasingly powerful technologies with as email, SMS, WhatsApp, voice broadcasts, direct mail marketing, etc

- And all you need is...a marketing automation platform!

Other benefits of marketing automation include:

- Total flexibility! Because the automation runs for you, you can work when you feel like it. You can get up as early or as late as you want - no more alarm clocks. You can take days off whenever you feel like it.

- You don't have to deal with hiring, training, managing and firing staff. Once you setup marketing automation for you, *it just gets the job done.*

- Marketing automation doesn't take sick days, get holiday allowance have maternity/paternity leave and doesn't go on strike either. In fact, *marketing automation is your best employee ever.*

- Marketing automation does a perfect job for you, every time. Because you can set it up to automatically send a welcome email to a new client, you can write multiple drafts of that email until it's just right to send. Unlike an employee who may make mistakes in going through the phone script, the software will send the perfect welcome email every time.

- You can spend more time with your loved ones, your family, your friends by outsourcing your sales and marketing to technology and not having to spend long hours in a specific office location.

- You can travel any time you want, visiting different countries.

- You can go to seminars, take a course, learn new things, expand your horizons.

- You can give yourself a pay raise every month. Increase your earnings every month, simply by perfecting your marketing automation and growing your email list!

"B2C marketers who leverage automation have seen conversion rates as high as 50%."

eMarketer

7.   What The Online Marketing Wizards Don't Want You To Know

Yes, there is a lot of "digital marketing wizardry" going on behind the scenes and as such there are "secret fraternity groups" that are behind many of the digital marketing success stories in the twenty-first century. And yes, there are a few things you would rather not know (or even think about) as they perform their wizardry rituals. This book is the first of its kind to actually a) reveal what is going on behind the scenes and b) simplify such acts of wizardry for the smart entrepreneur to benefit from.

Let's be clear. Some of those wizards are actually evil. Most bring valid "magic tricks" to the show. Many do guide people to treasure. I, for one, have been initially guided to treasure by one such "wizard". In most cases however, there is a discernible pattern behind everything they say, do and sell: a lack of solid ground. Most of their revenues is generated from the "teaching of the thing" rather than the "doing of the thing". This book doesn't just focus on magic tricks, but rather focuses on the core strategies to have in place to build and scale any business that wishes to profit from the internet.

It is in fact in the wizard's best (and economic) interest for you to believe that everything in the online marketing and business world is new; unaffected by the old principles of marketing and direct response.

Last but not least, it's in the wizard's interest to show you that today's shiny new trick is many times more profitable, shinier and superior than yesterday's trick.

This book is different. Whilst teaching you a few select "shiny" secrets, it shows you how to benefit from the huge opportunity that online marketing presents to any business. The teachings are based on the solid ground, proven tactics of direct response marketing adapted to the online marketing world. It is **your responsibility** to resist the seduction of short-lived, shiny lures, peer pressures and the siren-songs of superficially knowledgeable promoters of "new" tactics.

I taught myself (and practice) online marketing as a science and as a business, not as hobby. Many people (and their families) depend on the principles and techniques in this book. Mistakes can be costly not just economically but also from a human standpoint. In my roles as a strategic digital marketing coach I am all about creating advertising, marketing and business assets of lasting value for my clients - not moneymaking devices written in disappearing ink.

8.   Is This Book A Fraud?

This is, in one way only, a "fraudulent" book. The title is deceptive. It is indeed a book about the customer and prospect follow up, however this is not all it is about.

This is a proven playbook for growing a company that has effective lead generation and sales/conversion methods, both online and offline. Don't go into this book in a magpie-esq search to the next silvery, new, cool, quick, easy "fix" or clever gimmick – the one that might make you money today but require you to find another, and another and another, at frantic pace forever more.

Go into this book in search of deep understanding and profound clarity about the science of effective email marketing automation and how it can be applied to your business.

SECTION 2

THE MAGIC OF FOLLOW UP

1. How Can You Can DOUBLE Your Business?

Students often ask me "I promoted my product to XYZ people but why aren't they buying?" The answer is simple:

*People buy when **they** are ready to buy, not when **you** are ready to sell.*

There are a number of reasons why a prospect may come into contact with your business. In a minority of cases, those reasons will be strong enough for your prospect to buy whatever it is that you are selling. Those are typically the innovators and the early adopters.

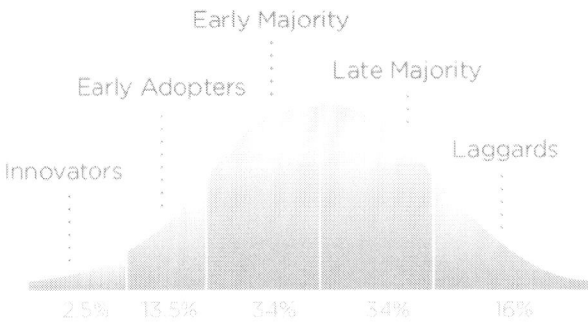

INNOVATION ADOPTION LIFECYCLE

43% Open Rates And 20% Conversion Rate

Milk&More deliver milk and other dairy products to over 1 million homes in the UK. As more and more of their orders are placed online, they realized their one-size fits all "spray and pray" approach to email marketing wasn't yielding the expected results. They created 3 automated email follow up campaigns:

- **Activation:** If someone signs up for Milk&More but does not place an order within 5 days, they are sent a Selling Campaign that includes a voucher for a discount off their services.

- **Welcome:** Once a customer has placed their first order, they will be entered into the Welcome Campaign urging them to place an ongoing order.

- **Lapsed:** For those who have not recently placed an order, Milk&More created a Nurture Campaign program to incentivize them place another order.

The results?

- The Selling Campaign (activation) averaged open rates up to **50%**

- **1 in 5 customers** became repeat customers thanks to the Welcome Campaign

- **20%** of lapsed prospects placed another order!

Find out more about Milk&More's story here:
http://ItsTheFollowupStupid.com/milkmore

In the majority of cases, those reasons might be strong enough to get the prospect to get in touch with you, but they would not be strong enough to get him to buy from you there and then. In this case, your business is ready to sell, but the buyer is not ready to buy. It's not that they don't like you or your business, it's not that there's something wrong with the product or the market, it's just that the prospect isn't at that point in the Buy/Sell cycle where they are ready to make a decision (I talk about this in detail in video 2 of my Covert Selling Formula program at <u>CovertSellingFormula.com</u>).

This is where email marketing automation comes into play with a follow-up series, which allows you to keep in regular contact with the prospect and progress him or her through the buying cycle up until the point where they are ready to buy. Up until that point, email marketing automation will also ensure that your business is TOMA, or Top Of Mind Always.

Nurturing and progressing the prospect through the buying cycle allow you to capture the sale, when the time is right.

What if you try to sell too early? You will only make a small percentage of the potential revenue because only a few prospects will be ready to buy that early in the buying cycle. You will fall in that category of people who are offering a perfectly fine offer to a perfectly fine audience and are complaining that conversions are not there. As the title of this book suggests, it's not the offer, it's not the audience, it's not the economy or anything else..."It's the follow up, stupid!".

"81% of conversions happen after the 5th marketing touch."

National Association Of Sales Professionals

How Morgan Brown Is Making $4,000/month Thanks To A Website "Incident"!

Morgan Brown was working for a mortgage company in the US in the mid-2000s when he discovered a true passion for writing and helping homeowners with the challenges they face around mortgages.

Within a year he was receiving 1 million visitors to his blog but suddenly the site went down due to a 3rd party attack.

Morgan had been collecting emails through the blog but had never actually sent a newsletter out to his subscribers. To make up for the lost traffic, we wrote a 6-email automated follow up sequence and sent it out through Aweber, which increased his revenues by $2,000 per month. After discovering the power of email follow up, Morgan wrote more follow up sequences eventually generating $4,000 per month from email marketing alone!

Find out more about Morgan's story here:
http:// ItsTheFollowupStupid.com/morganbrown

Now, let me ask you: "How many times do you consistently follow up with your prospects and customers on average?" I bet it's not more than 5 times. By having email marketing automation in place, you can sleep well at night knowing that you are capturing up to 81% more revenue for your business, *automatically.*

2. Is This The Best Investment You'll Ever Make?

There is abundant research showing that for every dollar spent on follow-up marketing and marketing automation, the average return is between $40 and $42 (the Direct Marketing Association publishes one such report on a yearly basis and the results are extremely consistent year in, year out). In essence, *for every dollar utilized, the average return is at least a 4,000% return on investment*! There is no other form of marketing or advertising out there that can command such a return!

As the majority of the profits in any business are in the back end, then having automated email marketing is the number one way to ensure that you are acquiring as many customers as possible which will in turn maximize your back end profits. Remember the 80/20 Rule? Search engine optimization and PPC might be a great way to draw people to your business at first, but following-up is the key to getting that 4,000% ROI and capturing that extra 81% of customers who are not ready to buy right away.

£198.40 From Every £1 Invested Thanks To Automation

Due to the competitive pressures in the market, the board of UK insurer Liverpool Victoria asked its marketing team to increase the number of policies sold whilst reducing the marketing budget.

Thanks to marketing automation, they set automated follow up emails to be sent to prospects and customers based on what type of policy they were interested in purchasing and their stage in the buying cycle.

For example, emails were sent 24 hours after the user abandoned the buying journey, then if a user did not return to the site and complete their purchase within three days a follow-up email ('retrieve your quote') was sent.

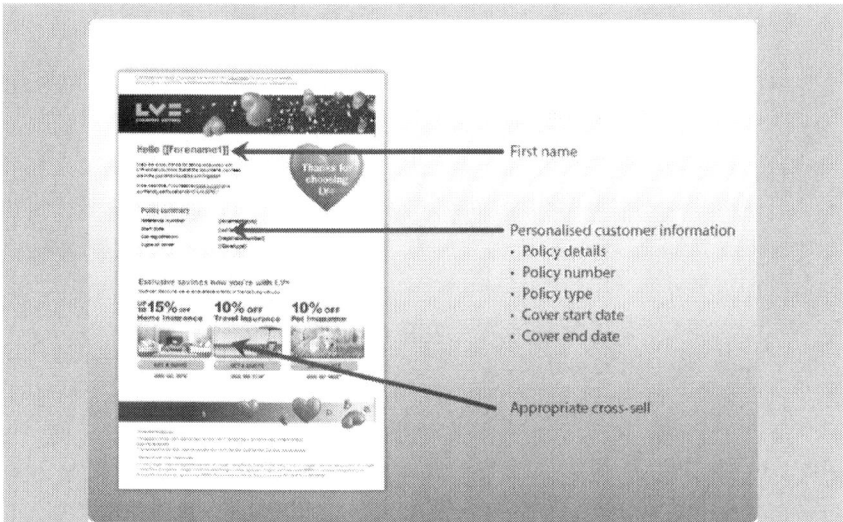

Another was an automatic "thank you" email which was sent after a purchase, with the intention to upsell those who bought.

The results? Impressive.

- Average monthly **open rate**: 51.1%
- Average monthly **click through rate**: 41.83%
- Average monthly total **customer conversion rate**:18.82%

Overall LV= made **£198.40 for every £1** that it spent on the new email strategy.

Find out more about LV's story here:
http://ItsTheFollowupStupid.com/liverpoolvictoria

10 Extra Holidays Per Year Thanks To Marketing Automation!

For Jim Turner, Optibike is an extension of his life as a motocross rider, tri-athlete, and semiconductor design engineer. For his customers, Optibikes are a great way to lose weight, commute without a car, and have fun. After buying his first electric bike in 1996, Jim found that it didn't climb hills or go far enough. So he decided to make a better one. He built his first model in 1998, and started Optibike in 2008.

"As a result of our automated sales funnel and tagging capabilities, we're now tracking every lead's progress, then creating tasks for sales floor follow-up and ongoing communication", says Jim Turner, Owner of Optibike.

The results?

- **Grew sales** from $532k to $1.45m
- **Increased leads** by 83%
- **Added** 10 vacation days per year

Find out more about Optibike's story here:
http://ItsTheFollowupStupid.com/optibike

3.   People Buy from People They Know, Like and Trust!

Never forget that! Take it and store it somewhere in your memory or maybe even write it down. The best way to get people to know you, like you and trust you is to stay in contact with them and show them a level of long-term commitment unlike anything they've seen or experienced with your competitors. What better way to achieve this than by having automated email campaigns do all that for you?

Robert Cialdini And The 6th Principle Of Ethical Persuasion

According to psychologist Robert Cialdini, author of the book *Influence: the 6th Principle of Ethical Persuasion,* the main reason why somebody will buy from you is commitment. Yes, you read that right - commitment. If you show your prospects and customers extraordinary commitment and stay in touch through multiple points of contact over time, you are (consciously or subconsciously) giving them the level of certainty that they need in order to do business with you. People buy from people they know, like and trust!

I have generated over $2 million in sales in the last 4 years, and because I stayed in touch with my prospects and customers over the years, people are more willing to buy programs ranging from $5,000 to $36,000 that I have available. They know me, they like me and they trust me because I have been communicating with them over long periods of time. I have also been able to sell some of the businesses I have been involved in at a significant premium because of consistently nurturing the relationship with the audience. I would not have been able to do this without email marketing automation. Don't misunderstand me, this doesn't only apply to prospects but applies also to existing or past customers of yours. Don't forget that the majority of your profits come from your existing customers. From our statistics, it's 8 times easier to sell a more expensive product to an existing customer than it is to sell a less expensive product to a new customer.

From Poor Health Making $30/month To Great Health Making $30,000/month Using Automated Email Campaigns!

Tom Menditto went from making $30/month, suffering from ADHD and with very few clients to making $30,000/month with great health by applying automated email follow up to his offline business.

To introduce his concepts to prospective customers, Tom started a blog and used it to build a mailing list. Using automated email series such as the Welcome Program Tom can educate and build a relationship with his prospects from the moment they sign up to his list. Then thanks to automated campaigns such as the Selling Campaign, the selling is done hands-free as by the time someone comes in contact with his paid programs, the prospect already feels like they know and trust him!

He says, "Literally I went from 300 bucks to $30K/month in less than a few years by applying the core principles of how you build an **online sales funnel**."

Find out more about Tom's story here:
http://ItsTheFollowupStupid.com/tommenditto

4. How to Fire 60% of Your Salespeople and Still Double Your Sales

Anecdotal evidence from my students and seminars shows that on average more than 60% of a sales rep's time is spent *educating* the customer. That's not selling, that's just telling the prospects the same thing over and over before he can even get to the decision stage of the conversation. What if you could shortcut that investment in time and money? How much more effective would your sales efforts be?

Thanks to email marketing automation you have five choices. One; fire the bottom 60% of your sales force and keep revenue the same. As a result profits will skyrocket. The beauty about cost cutting is that every $1 saved translates directly into a $1 increase in your profits. Two; keep that 60% of your sales force so they can spend more time selling **more** to **more** customers and eventually growing your business' revenue.

A third way you can reduce 60% of your sales overhead and still double your business is by having an intimate understanding of who are the hot leads in your database and who are the tired ones. This is all possible thanks to list segmentation. Most unsophisticated businesses have a database of leads, and spend the same amount of marketing time and money on all of them, regardless of how likely that prospect or customer is likely to do business with them. It's what I call the "Spray and Pray Approach". They hope that eventually someone will bite and purchase. With the amount of marketing automation technology now available (at such low costs) there is no other way of saying this other than...this is stupid!

So how else can you reduce your sales overhead by 60% and still double revenue? The fourth way is through **lead qualification.** This is what helps us to narrow down the 20% of our prospects who will generate 80% of our profits. Lead qualification is the process of asking a prospect a few critical questions before they even get into your database. These will allow you to immediately estimate how likely this person is to buy from you and therefore allows you to make an informed decision on how much time and money you want to spend selling to this prospect. These questions typically revolve around 3 aspects:

1. Does the prospect have a need for your solution?

2. Do they have an urgent need?

3. Do they have the budget for your solution?

The fifth way of reducing the amount of resources you invest in sales is **lead scoring**. As the business grows, naturally your database of leads grows. This means that some people who might be extremely engaged and interested in what you have to offer might become disengaged and disinterested later on (and vice versa). Things happen in business and in life and levels of interest go up and down for people.

Lead qualification takes place as soon as the prospect joins your list, whereas lead scoring takes place during the lifetime that the prospect is in your list. It measures the how the prospect's levels of engagement with your business change over time. For example, someone may join your list because he's interested in a specific free report you're offering but then goes cold. A few months later something may change in his business and he may start to re-engage very actively with your business and he may be considering buying from you. Lead scoring allows you to capture when that prospect goes from cold to hot so you can sell to him at the right time, when he's ready to make that buying decision.

How do we find those leads who are bubbling up and evolving from unengaged to engaged subscribers and then to rabid buyers?

Thanks to automated email follow up the software can determine when a lead becomes hyper engaged by analyzing their behaviour over your email campaigns.

How many emails are they opening? How many times are they clicking on the links within the emails? By analyzing all email behaviour, you can predict when a prospect is becoming particularly engaged with your offer or your product. As a result, you can send him a more targeted promotion. Do you have to do this every time someone goes from hot to cold? No, this can also be automated!

Thanks to lead qualification and lead scoring your sales efforts are not wasted across all leads but instead are targeted only on those prospects who are a) qualified and b) ready to buy from you.

British Reformed Telecoms Geek Makes $4,000 Recurring Revenue From A 500 Email List!

Adrian Savage is a 43-year-old self-proclaimed "reformed Telecoms geek" from Stoke-on-Trent in the UK.

Adrian developed a tool called WeDeliver.Email that allows users to improve their email deliverability, i.e. the number of emails that get delivered to the user's inbox instead of the spam folder.

Until September 2015, Adrian relied on referrals and promotions on social media groups to generate interest for this tool.

He then went on to create a lead magnet (eBook) helping users improve email deliverability. People can download it for free after entering their email address on a squeeze page. But he doesn't stop there. He also uses lead qualification and lead scoring to ensure he makes the most relevant offer to each one of his prospects as they come into pipeline.

After opting in, the visitor sees a page that asks him to choose the statement that best describes his situation. The page reads:

"Just one quick question before you go...

If you're an Infusionsoft user, I'd love to send you a few follow-up emails that will really help you stack the odds in your favour with deliverability and inbox placement. So that I can send you the right stuff, please choose the option that best describes you and press the Submit button:

- I send more than 10,000 emails a month using Infusionsoft

- I send fewer than 10,000 emails a month using Infusionsoft

- I don't use Infusionsoft, although I'm interested in using it

- I don't use Infusionsoft and just want to learn more about email deliverability"

"If they selected 'I'm interested in Infusionsoft', I contact them personally by email to offer them a one-to-one consultation.

If they selected 'More than 10,000 emails', they receive a series of educational emails reinforcing the most important parts of the lead magnet and offering a free trial of WeDeliver and a split test between Infusionsoft vs. WeDeliver.

If they selected 'Fewer than 10,000 emails', they just receive the educational emails and an offer for a free trial of WeDeliver.

If they selected 'I don't use Infusionsoft and just want to learn more about email deliverability', they also receive the educational emails series and may receive targeted affiliate offers down the line", says Adrian

Then, over the next few weeks using lead scoring he personally contacts those who have opened all of the emails or clicked on one of the links referring to a free trial or split test.

Prior to starting to build his list and implementing lead qualification and lead scoring, Adrian was averaging $1,000/month in sales from his software. After implementing email follow up and lead scoring and qualification, his revenues increased 4X. He's averaging $4,000/month in recurring revenue with a list of just 500 people!

Prior to starting to build his list and implementing lead qualification and lead scoring, Adrian was averaging $1,000/month in sales from his software. After implementing email follow up and lead scoring and qualification, his revenues increased 4X. He's averaging $4,000/month in recurring revenue with a list of just 500 people!

Find out more about Adrian's story here:
http://ItsTheFollowupStupid.com/adriansavage

Reduced Staff By Two Yet Increased Revenue 21%!

Tyler Smith started Select Photo-Graphics photo studio as a way to combine two things he loves—sports and photography. Tyler and Don were spending most of their time chasing down coaches in the hopes of scheduling a photo day. They would send hundreds of batch emails and leave countless phone messages just to glean a few willing leads. On the day of the actual photo shoot, much time was spent collecting checks and paper order forms, and a big chunk of the time after was spent fulfilling orders and keeping customers happy.

Instead of sending out those mass emails and leaving messages for coaches, Tyler and Don created an automated sequence to allow coaches to schedule a photo shoot on their own. And since coaches are notoriously slow to schedule, Infusionsoft would automatically send out some gentle reminders.

The results?

- **Reduced staff** by 2 people
- **Grew revenue** 21% in the first year
- **Increased leads** from 200 to 19,576 with the same ad spend
- **Spent** 15 more vacation days with family

Find out more about Select Photo-Graphics' story here:
http://ItsTheFollowupStupid.com/selectphoto-graphics

Email marketing is the most practical way you can reach your prospects and customers. How overwhelming would it be for the salesperson and the recipient to make and receive five, seven or eight sales calls selling your product? How much more natural, elegant and cost-effective to send the same number of emails instead?

5. Four Problems, Four Mistakes and One Big, Fat Lie About Email Follow Up

1) Lack Of...

The first mistake many people make is they spend a lot of time and money acquiring leads, creating the perfect product and putting together the perfect team, but once all of that is in place...they forget to follow up to close the sale!

> 81% of sales take place after the 5th marketing follow up, with an additional 10-12% taking place after the 10th follow up.
>
> *Reed Business, CSO Insights, Gartner, IDC, and Forrester Research as compiled by InsideSales.com*

Yet...

> 66% of the time business owners and their employees stop after just one or two points of contact. A staggering 92% gave up before the fifth contact!
>
> *MarketingDonut.com*

Other studies also found that if you communicate consistently with the prospect over a twelve- month period, your chances of converting that person go up by 61%.

Why is there lack of follow-up?

Things can get very busy, very quickly in business and entrepreneurs often rely on people to follow up. People are generally not as disciplined as artificial intelligence though and they will tend to only follow up once or twice. After that, whether they are the business owner or the salesperson, new issues and opportunities will arise and they often move on to the next thing on their list.

Many people become demoralized or busy with other tasks after making the first points of contact. This is where marketing automation excels! It will follow up five, six, seven, even eight times or more at virtually no cost. It will follow up 100% of the time -potentially an unlimited amount of times - so that you can focus on serving clients and building your business.

38% Boost In Sales With Marketing Automation!

When Debbie Green and her daughter-in-law created Minutes Matter in California, USA, they quickly became the leading provider for easy-to-use interior design software, quoting solutions and organizational systems.

Thanks to automated email follow up and Infusionsoft, they increased sales by 38%.

"If we hadn't started with Infusionsoft when we did, with the economy like it was, I'm not sure where we'd be today."

Debbie Green, Co-founder of Minutes Matter

Find out more about Minutes Matter's story here:
http://ItsTheFollowupStupid.com/minutesmatter

60% Boost In Sales With Automated Emails

When Julie couldn't find an aisle runner she loved while planning her wedding, she did what many entrepreneurs do: she created her own solution in her hometown in NJ, USA.

The Original Runner Company quickly became popular with media and celebrities for their unique non-slip, high-quality aisle runner designs. But with a "system" that consisted of index cards stored in a box, founder Julie Goldman needed a better way to communicate with brides-to-be throughout the long sales cycle.

Automated email follow up campaigns trigger once a prospect has requested a quote. The results?

- A 60% boost in sales

- Expanded follow up database by 500%

- Boosted referrals by 80%

Find out more about Julie's story here:
http://ItsTheFollowupStupid.com/julieoriginalrunner

The Follow Up Paradox

Most businesses only follow up once or twice, yet the majority of customers aren't converting until after the fifth point of contact.

Emailing prospects an unlimited number of times; isn't this spam?

As long as the follow-up is relevant and contains high-quality content, then chances are that it won't be considered as spam by the recipient. How do you send relevant content to your mailing list? Thanks to marketing automation, you can analyze your subscribers' behaviour (what emails they opened, what links they clicked on) to understand what they're interested in and send them only the most relevant offers. There are more specific, practical techniques to avoid spamming your clients and prospects, which we will cover later in this book.

An Industry Expert's Story

I used to be part a Ryan Deiss private mastermind group that cost (at the time) $25,000 to join. There were business owners in that group who were generating tens and hundreds of millions of dollars a year, selling both online and offline. When Ryan Deiss asked all of them what happened after they started emailing their list of prospects every single day instead of every month or every couple of weeks, they all reported similar results. What were their results?

They reported that by emailing their list of prospects every single day, their revenues increased. Some by 10%. Some by 200%. But the key message was that every business' revenue increased. These were multimillion-dollar business owners who were willing to try something new, and guess what? It worked!

$100,000/yr Selling Fiction Books To Her Mailing List

After studying Theology at Oxford University in the UK, Joanna Penn went onto a very successful career with Accenture working in their offices in Europe, Asia Pacific, New Zealand and Australia.

Joanna was in what some call a "Golden Handcuff Job"; a job that pays so much that it's difficult to leave even if you hate it. Eventually she decided to pursue a public speaking career and wrote a book to help her get more, higher paid speaking gigs. Despite appearing on Australian national TV, the book didn't sell so she started a blog with the intention of collecting email addresses and using email follow up to sell her crime thrillers.

Thanks to being able to keep in touch with her readers through email follow up, she has gone onto becoming a New York Times and USA Today best-selling author. She also built a $100,000+ a year book publishing and coaching business.

Find out more about Joanna's story here:
http://ItsTheFollowupStupid.com/joannapenn

The Dangers of Perceived Indifference

It's always interesting to hear people say that they don't want to follow up with their prospects "too much", because they don't want to "spam" them or they don't want people in their list to unsubscribe. The fact is that when you follow up frequently, many of your clients and prospects will consider this to mean that you care. To them, you're staying in touch with them and you care about them becoming clients of yours. The number one thing that kills businesses is perceived indifference! Those business owners are simply not contacting their leads enough.

Several years ago a study was conducted by the Peppers and Rogers Group in the U.S., and it had some startling (although somewhat unsurprising) news. It found that the number one reason listed by people who stopped using a business's services, was – drum roll, please! – perceived indifference! It's not that they don't like you; it's not the product, the price or your website...

On a subconscious level, people feel that if you're not following up with them, you don't care. Deep down, people want to buy something because they want something exciting and new to happen. Better yet, they want it to happen today. They want to change their life today. They yearn for the rush and the excitement they get after making a purchase. Sales go up dramatically when you contact your prospects on a daily basis. Try it like the business owners in the Deiss' private mastermind did - chances are that as a result your revenues will increase as well.

Maybe in your industry, contacting your customers and leads on a daily basis wouldn't be relevant. Maybe contacting them on a weekly basis is more suitable. Regardless, the advice is the same. **Be relevant to your audience. Email more.**

2) Not Seeing Email Marketing As...

"I love my email list" - "It's like magic, it really is"

Fran Kerr had a stable job as a government worker until she discovered her passion for all things nutrition and started a blog as a hobby, which then allowed her to build a mailing list of people interested in improving their nutrition. She then went on to write an eBook on "How to get rid of acne through diet" which she promoted to her email list.

"I love my email list", she says, *"and that's the main way that I sell the eBook even now. I sell it through the email list. It really has been the most successful thing for me in making money, because it's been a really great tool for promotion for everything that I sell...*

Even when I was out running this morning – this is really bad and shows me how addicted I am to email – I take my iPhone with me because I listen to music, so I was running and I was coming home, and often when I'm coming home I check my email on my iPhone. I had four book sales, because I've got two books now, and I noticed it in my email. I went, "Great! I sold four books last night in my sleep. How awesome is that?" It's like magic, it really is, says Fran.

Today Fran brings in anywhere from $4,000 to $12,000 a month income thanks to her business, and best of all she's living the dream of being in charge of how she leads her life and makes money doing something she loves.

Find out more about Fran's story here:
http://ItsTheFollowupStupid.com/frankerr

Most will agree that things like Search Engine Optimization (SEO), Pay Per Click (PPC) or offline advertising are some of the biggest sources of sales. If you spend $10,000 on a PPC campaign and makes $20,000 in return sales, then, generally speaking, that is a good ROI.

But, how about getting more sales out of your existing database of leads and customers? Business owners tend to be concerned with things like, how many new leads they get in a week, or how many new sales did they make that week? They're not asking themselves the questions that really matter. How about all those leads they already paid for but who haven't yet converted? How about generating more repeat business out of existing clients? How about following up with them with automated email campaigns over time so that your email marketing alone becomes a consistent source of revenue?

There's a good chance that some of your best clients and prospects (the twenty percenters) will be overlooked and forgotten about if you don't use email marketing automation. Remember how much potential and how important that seemingly small percentage of people is? The majority of the profit and the growth in your business will come from those prospects and customers. You need them to grow your business.

The most simple, most cost effective, yet most methodical way to keep a regular flow of sales transactions flowing through your business is through email.

3) No _____ And No _____

Remember when we said you should be emailing your list more often, but shouldn't be spamming them? The strict legal definition of spam is sending people **unsolicited** commercial email. Truth is that there is no real definition of spam. Someone, a client or a lead, might have requested commercial emails from you at some point, which means that technically you're not spamming that individual. However, that person can still consider (and flag) your email as spam.

> The real definition of spam is whatever the recipient considers to be spam, regardless of whether he or she opted in.

Consciously or unconsciously, a lot of marketers spam their list because they have **no personalization and no segmentation** in their email follow up strategy.

So, how do you avoid spamming your list?

Spam is primarily made of two elements: a lack of personalization and a lack of segmentation. Put together, this means not sending a message that is personalized to the recipient in relation to the data you have about them.

Segmentation is also is central to building a relationship of trust and value with your subscribers by sending content that is specific to that person's interest and behaviour over time. Rather than sending a message that *hopes* to apply to anyone and everyone, you're now having a direct conversation with the subscriber. Segmentation helps subscribers feel that they are part of a business that truly cares about their success and truly cares about making a difference to them rather than feeling that they are part of a mass marketing campaign.

What are a few examples of personalization?

The most basic type of personalization is first name and last name, contact email address, postal address or products they purchased. Another form of personalization could be something like, "Hi John, I noticed that you recently purchased *The Seven Days to Fitness*. You might be interested in our advanced workshop." In this instance, we are personalizing that message by inserting their name and the product name that they've purchased.

Another example is, if someone buys a motorcycle helmet from your site, to personalize that email with his name, details about his last purchase and other bike accessories which he might be interested in so that it will make that email feel more personal to him.

These are all forms of personalization. A more advanced type of personalization that can be done is personalization based on language, i.e. asking your subscriber to choose which language he prefers to receive communication in.

Another form of personalization is customizing specific *sections* of the email based on subscriber interests. If I'm interested in mountain biking and you are interested in cooking classes, we may both receive an email that gives us an update about the company. This email might say something along the lines of, "We've launched a new product recently that you might be interested in." Then, there will be a section in the email that has a Read More option personalized with content each of us are specifically interested in about. My email would link to something about mountain biking. You might receive the same email but that section will automatically populate with content about cooking classes. This is marketing at its best and it can be automated!

Emails can also be personalized geographically. So imagine receiving an email with a subject line saying, "Hello, George in Vienna." This would be very personal, and they're much more likely to engage with that email if it's relevant to their country or city. Personalization like this has been responsible for significant uplifts in open rates, click through rates and overall sales for my businesses as well as for my private clients.

How can you segment your list?

There are a number of different types of segments that we can build. Here are a few examples:

- **Interest**- over the last two months, three months or six months, what type of content has the subscriber shown interest in?

- **Activity**- have they engaged with your emails every day? Have they engaged with our marketing activities on a weekly basis or do they prefer to engage only once a month?

- **Source**- this is often overlooked. Leads coming from different types of sources will behave differently, so it's extremely important to store in our database the lead source so that we can communicate in the way that is most appropriate for that specific lead source. For example, a lead coming for a Facebook PPC ad will behave differently to a lead coming from a Facebook Fan page, which will in turn behave differently to a lead coming from a third party email promotion.

A lack of segmentation is characterized by not sending the right message to the right person at the right time (the "email trinity" as I like to call it). How do you avoid this? You can avoid this by segmenting your list across interests (city biking vs. mountain biking), purchasing behaviours (regular vs. seasonal) as well as demographics like age, sex, marital status etc.

You can analyze which groups of people tend to open a certain type of email. If there's a specific segment who always open emails that have the word "video" in the subject line, and tend not to open other emails, then you can create a segment that's only interested in receiving content in video format. If there's another segment of people who are only clicking on the links in your emails when there is a special discount code involved, then we know that segment of people is only interested in special offers. You can also analyze which people tend to open emails mostly on weekends so you can email them on weekends only. Sounds too complex? Any good email marketing automation platform can do the heavy lifting for you.

"From $600 to $19,000 Thanks To List Segmentation"

Miso Mlakic is a 32-year old software engineer from Croatia who went from making $600 from his 4,000 subscriber email list to $19,000 thanks to list segmentation.

He entered the email marketing world in a "conventional" yet smart way by building a list. Miso started sending traffic to a "squeeze page" asking people to enter their email address in exchange for downloading a free lead magnet. Once the visitor opted in, he would then present him with a related paid offer followed by an automated email series.

> He invested $5,000 on paid traffic (mostly solo ads) which yielded a list of 4,000 optin subscribers. At that point he stopped buying traffic and focused on building a relationship with his subscribers and monetizing the list.
>
> In order to do that Miso realized he had to analyze his list behaviour and segment it accordingly. As his autoresponder (Getresponse.com) didn't offer he features he needed he decided to take the matter onto his own hands and developed two Wordpress plugins that would achieve just that.
>
> "After doing my research and segmenting my list, I went from 4,000 people to about 700. I removed 3,300 subscribers in one day as I found out they were inactive. Quality of the list and relationship with it is what matters. Now I am focusing on my quality instead of quantity", says Miso.
>
> *You can learn more about Miso's plugins here:*
> *http://EmailExploder.com*

Over time, peoples' interests change, therefore we need to make sure that through segmentation, we are either confirming that person is still interested in that topic and, if not, where his interest is now. Email marketing automation would typically take care of all this automatically.

4) No _____ Equals No Sale

No follow up strategy equals no sale. A major mistake business owners make is not having a follow up strategy. The most common mistake I see made is that businesses send out a single email to an entire list and expect that to generate sales (and are often disappointed when that doesn't happen). Having a strategy means considering what type of content you are going to send, when you are going to send it, how you are going to send it and to whom you are going to send it. What is your editorial calendar going to look like? Are you sending educational content? Are you sending content about products? Are you sending special offers? Are you sending invites to webinars? Or, maybe a combination of those? Having the answers to all these questions is crucial before you even start to write the first word in your email campaign.

Once you have the email marketing strategy in place, how is this going to sync up with what the sales team is saying on the phone (if you have one)? How is it going to sync with any events that you're running?

If, for example, you're looking at selling your business in three years' time, is this email marketing program just attracting short-term sales, or is this marketing program attracting the type of customers that are going to provide the most value for a potential investor in three years time?

> "Email marketing is the glue to all marketing efforts of the business."
>
> *Tiz Gambacorta*

A business typically has a number of marketing strategies in place. Some of them are online and some of them are offline. The follow up that email marketing can achieve is the glue that binds all of these together in the sense that out of all those strategies, email marketing allows two things: 1) following-up with all your leads, no matter the source, and 2) personalized, automated follow-up to all those leads.

We can personalize the follow-up as a function of whether the lead was acquired at a trade show or through a Facebook PPC campaign. This is highly recommended because the way we should talk to leads coming from different sources is extremely different; therefore applying the same type of marketing to online and offline leads might not work. This is where marketing automation comes in.

> **"RWE Smashed The Conversion Target By 267% Thanks To Automated Emails"**
>
> When German energy giant RWE planned to use automated emails to promote their services, they wisely decided that one email would not be enough. Recipients not opening the main email were to be sent up to two reminder mailings with varying subject lines, both of which offered an incentive.
>
> Recipients clicking on the offer but not successfully registering were to be sent a special reminder email prompting them to complete the process.

> The results? Just over one in ten recipients (11%) registered for the RWE 'Online Customer Account', far surpassing the original target of 3%.
>
> *Find out more about RWE's story here:*
> *http://ItsTheFollowupStupid.com/rwe*

5) Lack Of _____ Or Worse, _____

Lack of skills or worse, over-confidence. Everyone can send an email, but not everyone can send a marketing email that is engaging and that can result in more leads and more sales for your business. Many of us know how to engage with people one-on-one, but do you really know how to engage large numbers of people online? Do you really know how to engage people who don't know you personally? Do you really know how to engage people enough to get them to do business with you? Most importantly, do you know how to do all of these successfully by email?

When a business sends out an email last minute to their database and they don't see the desired result, that's a direct symptom of overconfidence. Instead of trying to do everything in-house for actions that require a specific skillset, why not get educated by experts in the field or work with an external partner who can guide you through what can quickly become a minefield?

"It's too expensive! I can send an email myself."

I often get that objection after speaking at events where I encourage entrepreneurs to leverage email marketing automation. If you think hiring a professional is expensive, try hiring an amateur! Hiring a professional might come across as a large investment up front, but if you try to do it yourself and it doesn't work for you (if you think you can do it, by all means, try!), then what is that going to cost you in terms of lost opportunities? Lost sales? What is that going to cost in terms of all those leads who haven't engaged with your communications and, as a result, end up speaking to a competitor and doing business with them instead?

> ### "Doubled Sales In 1 Year Thanks To Marketing Automation"
>
> Joe Stone from Swim Fitness in California, USA sells high end swim spas. After attending a seminar, Joe setup segmentation and automated email follow-up campaigns into his business. Thanks to marketing automation platform Infusionsoft, he also has the system automatically schedule a series of tasks for the assigned sales rep, including follow-up reminders.
>
> The results? Thanks to automated email follow up and marketing automation Joe doubled sales in 1 year!
>
> *Find out more about Joe's story here:*
> *http://ItsTheFollowupStupid.com/swimfitness*

A professional will most likely get it right, or at least get better results than a non-professional would on their own. What is that incremental investment worth to you, versus having to try and reinvent the wheel yourself?

6) Not Being Willing to Take ...

Not being willing to take that leap of faith. People don't like change, and we as business owners especially don't like it because it's risky. However one of our best decisions in business can come from the moments where we take a *leap of faith*. Before we've taken that leap of faith we've still probably thought to ourselves, "I understand all of this, I understand how it applies to other people's businesses, but what if it doesn't work for me? What if I make the investment and get bad results?"

Take that dive into the dark and try something new; it might just revolutionize the way you do business! How will you know if you don't try?

> "The definition of insanity is doing something over and over again and expecting a different result."
>
> *Albert Einstein*

If you want to grow your business and leave a legacy to the world - to change people's lives - don't expect it to happen unless you change the way you do things. Try something new so that you can get different results, reach your goals and leave behind a great legacy!

7) **Replacing Email With...**

Replacing Email with Social Media Communication. Out of the seven mistakes business owners often make, this is the newest one. With the growth of social media, there has been an increasing focus on shifting commercial communications away from email and into social media channels like Facebook or Twitter. Although these channels have a very important presence in the marketing mix, it's important to take a step back and look at how social media compares to email.

> 93% of online users have an email address whereas only 38% of users are friends with or following a brand on Facebook.
> *Kissmetrics*

For about every three people that have an email address, only one is actually communicating via Facebook with a brand. If we look at Twitter, the picture gets even smaller because only 5% of Twitter users follow a brand. And the best part is that if you look at social media giant Facebook, they are actually one of the largest senders of email globally!

What is the number one way Facebook re-engages a user?

The number one way Facebook reengages a disengaged user is... with email! Email is the glue that unites all Internet users (and marketing) worldwide, and it's the only channel that has the power to attract users - and bring them back to a website. No other channel can 'push' you to visit a site unless you first proactively log onto their portal.

73% of people check their emails first thing in the morning. So, if you want to be sure to reach your customer, email is always the way to go. Social media has a very important role in your marketing communications; however, don't replace email with social media. And the best part? Most businesses spend time, effort and resources on social media, PPC and SEO yet they don't have email follow-up! This is a huge paradox considering that email is one of the cheapest forms of communicating with clients, not to mention that it generates a 4,000% ROI year in year out!

8. Ignoring Unengaged Subscribers

Unengaged subscribers are often looked down upon by businesses on the general assumption that, if they're not engaging with your marketing communications, they're not likely to buy any of your products. What I found with a my businesses and private clients, is that unengaged subscribers are still generating revenue for businesses as a result of good automated email follow up. How is this possible?

This test was performed for a large client in the retail business with a database size of 8 million subscribers. The "unengaged" subscribers were isolated into a separate segment. An "unengaged" subscriber was defined as someone who didn't open an email in the last 60 days. 50% of the database was subjected to conventional marketing practices, i.e. they were not sent any email communications as they were deemed inactive. The other 50% was continued to be marketed with regular newsletters (the Nurturing Phase) over a 3 months period. Which group generated the most sales? The second segment that was receiving regular email marketing despite not opening the emails. Why is this? Despite the fact that they were not opening the company's emails, the study showed how the simple fact that they were seeing an email from the company in their inbox raised their brand awareness which prompted them to walk into the company's stores and purchase!

Even if they don't open it, even if they don't click on the email, the simple fact that they stay subscribed and see you in their inbox keeps you at the top of their mind. As a result, sales will increase for you! As we will cover in a later chapter, looking at traditional email marketing metrics such as open or click through rate can be misleading and extremely costly.

> "When is a subscriber truly dead? When they have stopped breathing."
>
> *Tiz Gambacorta*

6. Can Your Business Become An Industry Giant?

Artificial intelligence is changing the modern business landscape and companies need to evolve with the times in order to keep up. A study by University of Oxford suggests that nearly half of our jobs will be lost to computers in the next twenty years. That means that two out of every four working individuals' skills and abilities will become obsolete due to the rise of artificial intelligence. Unfortunately, a lot of people will be out of a job, but we also realize that businesses who are not able to keep up will be left in the metaphorical dust of their competitors.

Some of the companies with the greatest Internet presence use the advanced algorithms and marketing automation techniques we will talk about. Amazon, Google and Facebook all use similar techniques. The most powerful companies of our time track the clicks and movements of prospective customers and have mastered the art of personalized, automatic marketing. This is simple. This is also huge. We want to share it with you so that you can implement it into your own business. We want to share the best practices and cutting-edge ideas for you to get the most out of this technology. With the right software and a little bit of motivation, you can realize your financial goals and dreams. You can change the tide for your business once and for all AND you can get a head start on your competitors!

You have the potential to create a business with the similar levels of success of companies like Facebook, Amazon and Google. Let's not forget that these industry giants all started from the ground up. Facebook, when it became public, wasn't the only social networking site out there, but they did something that would set them apart from the rest. They became extremely good at analyzing user behaviour as users interacted with the platform and they took it a step further by keeping users engaged and connected with Facebook. They evolved into the massive, social stream of consciousness that they are today because they mastered the formula which we will discuss throughout this book. They made themselves into a company worth billions and, as you will come to find out, it isn't rocket science to boost your sales and your company's net worth so long as you use the right strategies and techniques.

Every day, companies like Amazon and Facebook initialize hundreds of what we call "split tests" (or A/B tests). These tests enable them to analyze consumer behaviour and market products and services to them accordingly. In other words, if we had 100 different people opening the same homepage, they would likely see a different page to one another. Every purchase you make on Amazon will determine the next items they will sell to you, and this is all based off of split tests and analysis to determine what you are interested in and what people who buy similar items are interested in. Because of the personalization in each suggested item, customers often end up purchasing more. This is marketing automation at its finest!

Let's not leave out Google; an entire business based on artificial intelligence, click tracking, split tests and discovering the most relevant information to people's searches that people want to view on websites. With Google, relevance is key to providing people with what they're looking for and to keeping a strong connection with their 1.17 billion users. Just ask one of their many users, and most of them will tell you that they would never use another search engine – so much so that the term "google it" has become the universally adopted way of saying, "search for it on the internet".

"Amazon's $300 Million Button"

Jared Spool of User Interface Engineering took Amazon's business to the next level to the tune of $300 Million with "simple" tweak that wouldn't have been possible if the company wasn't a huge fan of A/B testing.

Having a registration form for customers to complete before purchasing items was placed with the intention to capture the customer details for future relationship building. Whilst this sounds like a reasonable deduction, in actual fact they were putting a barrier in the way. Prospective customers didn't want to start a relationship at that stage... they wanted to make a purchase.

Jared removed the registration form before the purchasing page and this simple change alone saw revenues increase by a truly astounding $15 million the first month. !

> This equates to a whopping $300 million in the first year, not bad for just running an A/B test
>
> *Find out more about Jared's story here:*
> *http://ItsTheFollowupStupid.com/jaredspool*

Life simply would not be the same without these giants. And what made them stick out above all of their competitors? Laser-targeted, automatic marketing with a side of personalization. That is one potent dish!

If you're a business owner or a leader within an organization, ask yourself these questions:

- *How can you grow and keep competing without marketing automation?*

- *Can you keep hiring more and more employees to do the same manual jobs every day?*

It's likely that you won't be able to grow without marketing automation unless you are okay with your costs skyrocketing. Or, imagine you continue to hire more and more employees, paying double or quadruple the cost you would otherwise pay for a single, more efficient, more reliable and easier piece of technology to do the job for you. If you are really looking to speed up the growth of your business, or if you hope to eventually sell your business, or maybe even pass it on as a legacy to your predecessors, then marketing automation is simply inevitable.

7. Is The Most Profitable Part Of Your Business Also The Easiest?

The 80/20 Rule we discussed in the previous section is rather straightforward. In virtually any business, about 20% of your clientele will generate 80% of your sales. The other 80% of customers tend to be sitting ducks of sorts and, more often than not, they do not feel a sense of loyalty to your company, your brand, and your offers. It is not to say that these customers do not matter, but oftentimes businesses overspend trying to draw in the 80% who won't generate the sales volume they are looking for. This ends up costing more in terms of customer service, salespeople, expensive marketing campaigns, and so on and so forth.

Marketing automation and automatic email follow-up allow businesses to focus on the 20% who make a significant difference. The less serious customers (or rather, the 80%), can be segmented into a list that will still receive automatic follow up, yet the company will no longer overspend on marketing.

Using advanced algorithms and marketing automation technology I can help you IDENTIFY your top 0.8-4%, sell *more* to them, and identify more prospects *like* them, to double or triple your business while reducing your costs.

If you're wondering how I got to those numbers, 20% of your prospects will generate 80% of your revenues. Out of those 20% of prospects, 20% will generate 80% of the revenues. So 20% of the 20% (4%) will generate 80% of the 80% of the revenues (64%). Apply the same logic again and you find that 0.8% of your database generates more than 51% of your revenue!

I have been able to generate millions of dollars in sales because I learned that the majority of profits in any business come from the back end. The biggest mistake many businesses make is that management often neglects their established customer base and focuses on attracting as many new leads as possible. Remember the 80/20 Rule? Well, it applies directly to this too. Eighty percent of your sales will come from your existing customers. Your loyal customers. Can you afford to ignore the handful of people who will generate you the most business?

Having a marketing automation system in place allows you to keep your customer base engaged with the company and feel a level of involvement that they otherwise wouldn't feel. This does one very important thing: it lets our prospects and customers feel that they are *important* to you and your business. Let's emphasize this once more: **it lets our prospects and customers feel that they are important to you and your business.** Psychologically speaking, we as human beings have an overwhelming desire to feel cared for.

According to Maslow's hierarchy of needs, the need to feel love and belonging (intimacy) comes just after physiological (food and water) and safety (shelter and stability) needs. We as business owners often miss this important fact, and tend to forget that our customers and our leads are not just a name, or (even worse) a number on a list.

SECTION 3

THE FIVE PHASES OF SELLING WITHOUT SELLING

1. "I Don't Want To Be A Spammer"

When it really comes down to it, barely anybody actually enjoys the idea of selling – having to high-pressure, convince, connive, and overcome countless barriers of human psyche just to persuade another human to purchase what you're offering is a process that just sounds exhausting. It puts immense pressure on the person selling and on the person being sold to.

There's an image in our culture of the cheesy, grinning, checker-suited salesmen buzzing around like an annoying fly, offering deal after deal in a desperate attempt to make a sale until someone finally breaks, gives in, and forks over cash just so they'll be left alone. No one wants to be THAT person and nobody wants to be bothered by that person. We all have our dignity.

So, when it comes to email marketing and selling through email, the reoccurring (almost conditioned) thought process is "I don't want to be that desperate spammer".

Here's the thing – no effective salesperson, whether it be today or a hundred years ago - used those cheesy sales tactics. All of the best ones – the ones actually making fantastic careers about of their ability to sell and convince –did so without actively trying to sell anything to anyone at all.

2. How Can You Sell Without Selling?

> *"Personally I am very fond of strawberries and cream, but I have found that for some strange reason, fish prefer worms. So when I went fishing, I didn't think about what I wanted. I thought about what they wanted. I didn't bait the hook with strawberries and cream. Rather, I dangled a worm or grasshopper in front of the fish and said, "Wouldn't you like to have that?" Why not use the same common sense when fishing for people?"*
>
> *- Dale Carnegie, "How to Win Friends and Influence People"*

Dale Carnegie was perhaps one of the most prolific salesmen, speakers, and writers of the 20th century, and he learned very early on that if you want to sell something to somebody, the last thing you should do is try to convince them to buy. Instead, just listen and they'll convince themselves.

Selling without selling is a very simple concept and it breaks down to this:

1. Don't try to sell something to somebody who doesn't want it.

2. Listen more than you talk, and people will simply tell you what they want

3. Give people what they already want when they're looking for it

4. As a bonus – it helps to be patient.

The fisherman doesn't have to convince a fish to bite their hook – all a fisherman needs to do is bait the hook with what the fish already wants, go to where the fish already is, and dangle it in front of the fish when it is hungry.

Email marketing is no different.

*   People are opting in to receive emails from you because they're already interested in the content you're providing

- You are providing your email list with the exact kind of content and information they said they're already interested in

- You are selling products/services that directly align with what your list has already expressed that they want, desire, and believe they will benefit from

In this section we're going to go over the five phases of selling without selling, which are as follows:

1. The Welcome Phase – This is a (short) campaign sent directly after someone opts-in to your list for the first time welcoming them on board, building a relationship, establishing trust, and creating rapport.

2. The "Selling" Phase – This campaign is, as the name would imply, geared toward turning the people on your list into a converted sale (customer) for a specific product or service.

3. The Consumption/Retention Phase– It's not enough to just make a sale and walk away. Most of your success in marketing is going to come from people who have already purchased previous products. A consumption campaign continues to engage with people who have just purchased to ensure they are using your product and are happy about with it, ultimately reducing refunds, returns, etc. This phase also converts them from customers into raving fans for you and your brand.

4. The Grouping Phase – The biggest mistake you can make as an email marketer is to keep marketing the same things the same way to everyone on your list. A Grouping Campaign allows you to start segmenting your list based on their "digital body language" (aka what offers are they expressing interest in), so that you can craft highly-targeted emails that appeal directly to their immediate wants and desires.

5. <u>The Nurturing Phase</u> – Just because someone does not buy during a Selling Campaign, does not mean they will not buy the same product eventually (or a different product if you're offering multiple products/services). The best thing to do with these leads is continue to nurture them by providing valuable, relevant content over an extended period of time and then attempting to re-engage them later through a new Grouping Phase.

Over the next five chapters, we're going to delve into each one of these phases in more depth. Let's get started.

3. The Welcome Phase

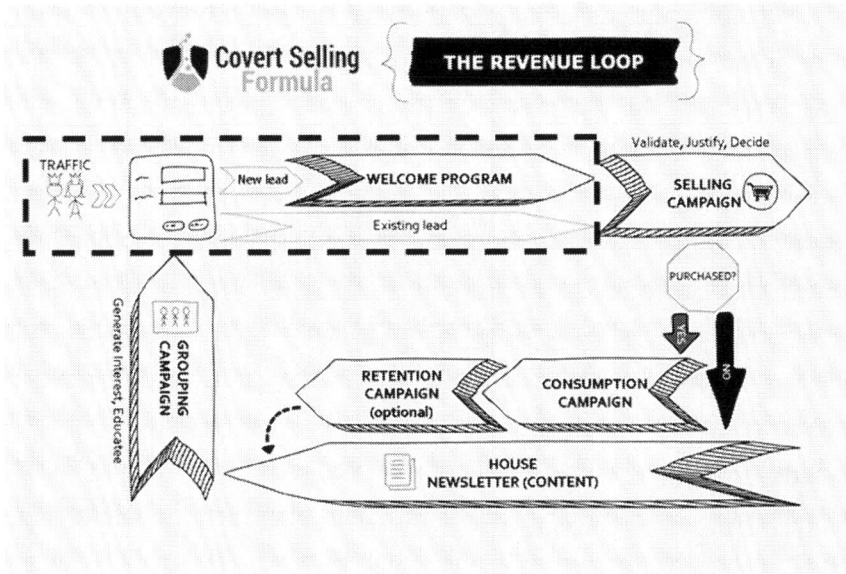

Many newbie email marketers end up making one of the following two mistakes when first starting out.

1. They get so caught up with how many people are opting in to their list, that they focus all their efforts on getting more opt-ins and no effort on welcoming or "onboarding" the people who already have opted in (and are potentially ready to buy from them).

2. They are so impatient and so desperate to sell something that they begin blasting out sales emails to every new opt-in without developing a trusting relationship with them first.

Both of these tactics are disastrous! If your leads don't physically opt-out of your list, they'll emotionally opt-out and simply ignore what you send.

A welcome phase is designed to warm up your leads, to tell them a little bit about you, what to expect from you, and also ask them about themselves using polls and surveys.

On the surface, this may not seem important for "closing the sale". However, the process couldn't be more vital for higher conversion rates and client loyalty down the road. Why?

1. **Desperation Stinks** – There are a lot of similarities between dating and selling, in either situation both people essentially know what the end goal is. If a guy asks a girl out on a date it's because he is physically attracted to her – she knows this. The end goal for either one of them is to eventually develop a romantic relationship (and everything that goes along with it). Yet, what's going to kill any chance of that happening is if the same guy comes on too strong – he will blow his chance of getting to the end goal by being too insistent. Likewise, if the girl becomes too clingy and desperate for devotion, the guy is going to get turned off. Why? Because even when either party knows the end goal, the evident desperation to achieve it pre-maturely stinks so bad it derails the process.

   What do people do on a first date? They get to know each other, they build up rapport, they learn each other's interests, and they establish a level of mutual comfort. By having no immediate requirements, both parties become more relaxed and, in the process, closer.

   This is no different between you and the leads on your list. Remember, these aren't just a bunch of nameless, faceless email addresses – these are real people with real personalities and they need to be courted and treated with respect before they jump into bed with your product or service.

   If you're too desperate to sell them, they'll smell it straight from their inbox. Sure, deep down inside they know that the reason they signed up to your list is because they're interested in what you're offering. And, sure, they know that the emails you send will eventually try to sell them on something. That doesn't mean that they don't want to be treated as a human being in the process, in which their opinions and feelings are both recognized and validated.

2. **Familiarity** – A welcome campaign helps your leads become familiar with your emails showing up in their inbox. They begin to recognize the sender (you) and they also begin to recognize that the emails you send hold value – non-threatening information that helps them solve the problem that caused them to sign up in the first place. When you do eventually shift to a sales campaign, they will be more likely to open your email rather than dismiss it.

3. **Listening** – There are a lot of things you can do with your welcome campaign aside from simply talking about your brand, preparing them for the type of emails they'll be sent, and sharing helpful information regarding your products and services, you can also ask your audience for their opinions and preferences, which can help you later on in the grouping phase (which we'll go over later) and give you valuable insight into your list. You can do this by sending surveys or polls. You can ask, for example, whether they're more interested in one product over another. You can ask them what kind of content they would like to receive in the future. You can ask them to prioritize the different problems that your solutions are seeking to solve. Even the people on your list who DON'T respond to a poll or survey, will still appreciate the fact that you asked – this shows that you value their opinion and time.

Every new lead that comes into your list should first be put on a welcome campaign that is at least two to five emails long over the course of one or two weeks (at this stage you'll be sending between one and three emails a week, ideally).

For example, here are a few emails from a welcome campaign for a natural diabetes cure newsletter. The Lead Magnet was a free eBook entitled, "The 10 Secrets to Curing Diabetes Naturally".

The emails start out simply enough – providing the book download (that they signed up for) and explaining that the lead is now on the email list while giving them both an idea of what to expect as far as content, as well as clear instructions of how to opt-out (this is important for anti-spam reasons).

> Hi <firstname>!
>
> Thanks for signing up for the free eBook, "The 10 Secrets to Curing Diabetes Naturally". You can download it by clicking the link below:
>
> [LINK]
>
> We'd also like to let you know that you've been signed up to receive more emails from us, in which you'll be receiving all sorts of vital and valuable information on how to cure diabetes naturally and live a natural, healthy life.
>
> If this isn't something you're interested in, just click "unsubscribe" at the bottom of this email and you will receive no further emails from us.
>
> However, if you're truly interested in crushing diabetes once and for all without the use of expensive doctor visits and drugs, stay tuned because we're going to send you information Big Pharma wishes you didn't know.
>
> Talk to you soon!

Next, the emails begin to educate or "indoctrinate" the lead, essentially building trust with useful free information and priming them to eventually buy in the next phase.

> Hi <firstname>, to some people it sounds like a crazy conspiracy theory, but one guy – Dr. Robert D. Young – has blown the lid off the pharmacy industry's big, bad secret – they WANT you to have diabetes!
>
> Seriously, they are literally banking off the fact that you have diabetes and even though you could completely reverse

your diabetes in less than 21 days naturally, it's simply more profitable for you to stay sick.

Big Pharma draws in $215 BILLION selling products that do nothing but treat your symptoms and get you hooked on drugs that make you worse, not better. They want you to be 100% dependent on their meds and they don't want you to know that you can become whole again without their drugs.

Click below to read our new blog on how you can…

- *Get off the drugs*

- *Throw away the needles*

- *Stop the embarrassment*

- *Obliterate your diabetes in just 21 days*

[LINK]

Don't let big pharma convince you that you need their drugs – you don't.

Talk to you soon.

As you can see here, the email is continuing to provide valuable information (and encouragement) without asking for anything in return. This should continue on for a few more emails until you're ready to move onto the next phase.

In fact, if you've provided a Lead Magnet such as an informational case study, white paper, or eBook, you may also want to "check in" with them and see if they have any questions and so on to give a really personal touch.

Once you get about two to four welcome emails sent, it's time to move onto the next phase – selling.

4. The "Selling" Phase

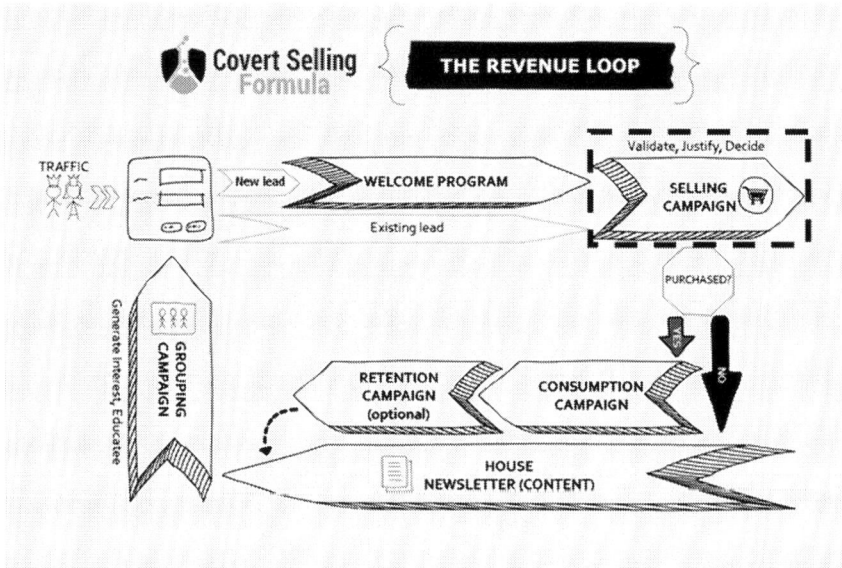

By now you've warmed your audience up through a welcome campaign, you've gotten them used to receiving emails from you, and you've (hopefully) gained some insights into their behaviour.

At this point, you can start "selling". Why the quotation marks? Because by the time the prospect gets to this stage he already expressed his interest about our offer (by opting in for a Lead Magnet) and is already educated about who we are and what we can do for him. In other words, by now he's a) interested in our offer and b) knows us, therefore, the "Selling" phase is simply helping the subscriber make that decision whether our solution is the right for him.

Okay STOP.

Wait a second before your fingers get too itchy and you send out that "buy now" email.

Just because you are ready to enter into a Selling Campaign, doesn't give you license to blast out high-pressure sales emails. There is an important, delicate process you should go through.

In keeping with a "selling without selling" philosophy, the number one thing you should remember with a Selling Campaign is that your job isn't to write emails trying to convince anybody to buy anything, nor is your job to write emails talking about how great your product is. This is just going to result in physical and emotional opt-outs.

Instead, your job is to prime them for a sale and then provide them the ability to purchase what you've already primed them to buy. See the difference? ;)

For example, let's say your product is a chew toy for dogs that helps dogs clean their teeth and keep their breath fresh.

Rather than sending out an email urging your leads to buy this new chew toy or an email talking about how great it is, it would be better to follow a formula similar to the following (courtesy of Infusionsoft):

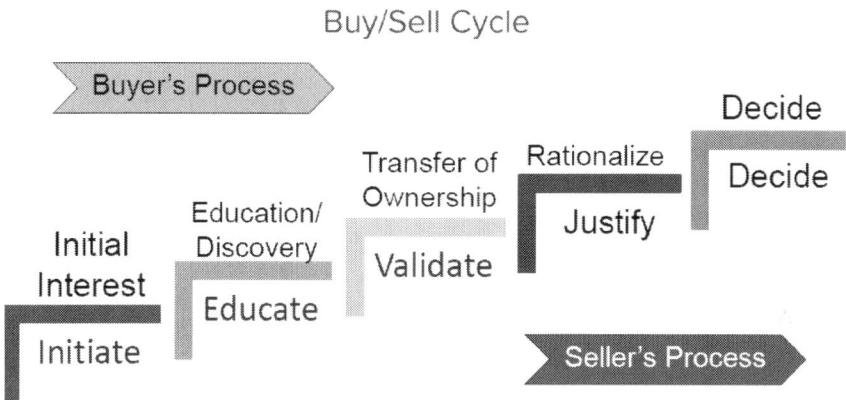

Buy/Sell Cycle

Buyer's Process

Decide
Decide
Transfer of Ownership
Rationalize
Justify
Education/ Discovery
Initial Interest
Validate
Educate
Initiate
Seller's Process

A roadmap for action. It helps ensure that you use the right tool at the right time and is a vitally important way to retain control during the sales cycle.

- **Email One** – "Does Your Dog Have Bad Breath?" write about what causes dogs to have bad breath, and some natural solutions to help solve the problem.

- **Email Two** – "Should You Brush Your Dog's Teeth?" talk about the pros and cons of brushing your dog's teeth as well as how to do it

- **Email Three** – "Can Bad Doggy Breath Mean Digestive Problems?" write about how stomach problems can sometimes cause bad breath and how to make sure your dog's digestion is on point through correct diet.

There are a couple of tactics you can use with these emails in order to sell your product.

1. **Provide the offer with a CTA at the end of each email** – In this case, you provide valuable information (such as natural ways to cure bad breath in dogs) and then include your product at the end as one of those natural ways (maybe even with a percent off coupon code). This could be done on all the email examples listed above. For example, "If your dog has bad breath, our Breezy Breath Chewy Toy will eliminate bad breath while providing your dog with hours of play time."

2. **Send one to three sales emails at the end of these "selling prep" emails** – Instead of providing an offer within the emails, you could send out two or three prep emails and then send out two or three emails after that as pure sales emails. For example, email one could say something to the effect of, "We've gotten so many people interested in solving their dog's bad breath, we decided to put X Product on sale for the next 72 hours only" and then proceed to list the benefits. The next email could be a reminder 24 hours after that, with the final email showing up one hour before the "sale" is supposed to end. Of course, you can re-do this sale a month later if you wanted. Or even extend it saying something like, "When the sale ended I had a flood of emails from people who weren't able to take advantage, so I've decided to extend it another 24 hours just in case you missed it!"

These sales campaigns are "selling without selling" because they are essentially providing useful information on solving a problem – information that your leads have already opted-in to receive in the first place.

If you follow this section correctly, you will make some solid sales. However, this is in no way the end of the process as it is incredibly important to nurture your current customers in the Consumption Phase, which we'll cover in the next section.

5. The Consumption Phase

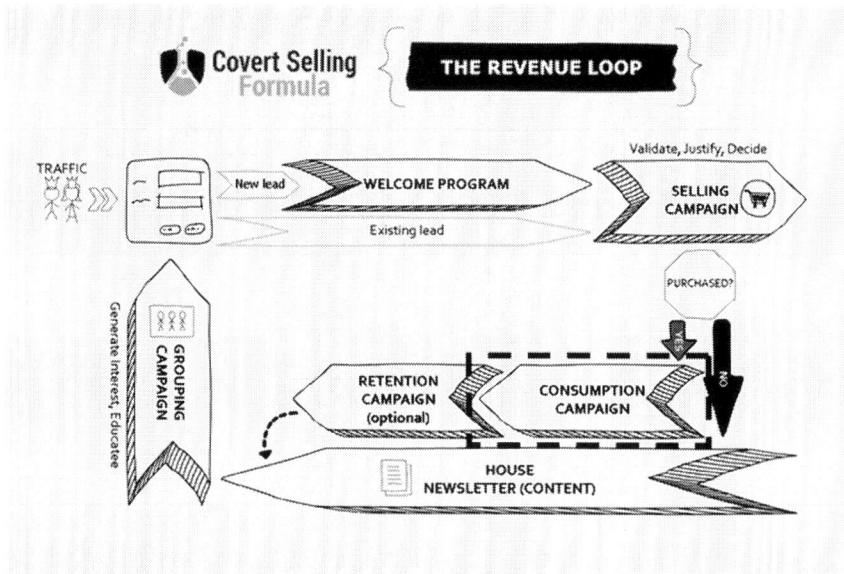

This is perhaps the most important aspect of the five phases of selling without selling while also being the most neglected. Even some of the most sophisticated digital marketers out there make the mistake of simply skipping this phase all together.

The Consumption Phase is essentially a customer retention strategy – it's a tactic that allows you to nurture people who have already converted into customers.

First, let's look at why it's so incredibly important to nurture this group of people:

- It costs six to seven times more to acquire a new customer than to retain an existing one (Bain & Company).

- Current customers are also vastly more likely to buy again. You have a 10% to 30% chance of converting a new prospect into a sale (at best). You have a 60% to 70% chance of converting an existing customer into a repeat customer (*Marketing Metrics: The Definitive Guide to Measuring Marketing Performance*, Paul W. Farris).

- 80% of your future profits will come from just 20% of your existing customers (the 80/20 rule, as originally presented by Vilfredo Pareto and further elaborated by Perry Marshall in his book *80/20 Sales and Marketing*).

- Increasing customer retention rates by <u>just</u> 5% will increase profits between 25% and 95% (Bain & Company)

Yet, even with this knowledge, 55% of marketing efforts are spent solely on acquiring NEW customers (McKinsey & Company)!

Many marketers would rather disappear after they make a sale in order to concentrate on converting new leads, than to continue following up with customers to maximize profits.

This is essentially what the Consumption Phase is all about – it ensures that your buyer consumes the product they just purchased, that they are happy with the product and last but not least, it helps you turn that person from "just" a customer into a raving fan for you and your business.

Here are a couple of examples of the Consumption Phase in action:

- You sell a training course on how to gain more respect in the workplace, so you initiate a consumption campaign that ensures your customers are understanding the information and applying it correctly.

- You sell a new natural cleaning product that gets harsh stains out of carpets, so you send information on the best ways to use the product on specific types of stains and specific types of markers and you send polls/surveys asking about their results removing the stains.

A side benefit of an effective Consumption Campaigns is gathering customer testimonials. Real, authentic testimonials are invaluable. It not only provides social proof for your products and services, it tells your customers that you value their input.

Here's an example of a testimonial gathering email.

> *Hey <firstname> - you did it!*
>
> *You officially made it to day thirty of The 30-Day Fitness Challenge. It's been a wild ride, and very challenging at times, but together we've made it through to the finish line and I hope you're feeling as great as we are!*
>
> *In fact, we'd love to hear how great you feel! As you know, we're always looking to inspire people all over the world to get the lean, fit body they've always wanted and it's people like you that provide the most encouragement.*
>
> *Because of that, we would love for you to send over your honest testimonial as well as your before/after pictures so that we can post them on our site (with your permission of course), as well as social media, in order to inspire others just like yourself.*
>
> *Not only does this help inspire others, it lets us know if there's anything that we can improve upon or do better.*
>
> *We're proud of you, and we hope YOU'RE proud of you.*
>
> *Looking forward to hearing about (and seeing) your amazing transformation.*

But let's take a step back...what do you do about those people on your email list that didn't convert into a sale? Do you just ignore them or remove them from your list?

6.   The Nurturing Phase

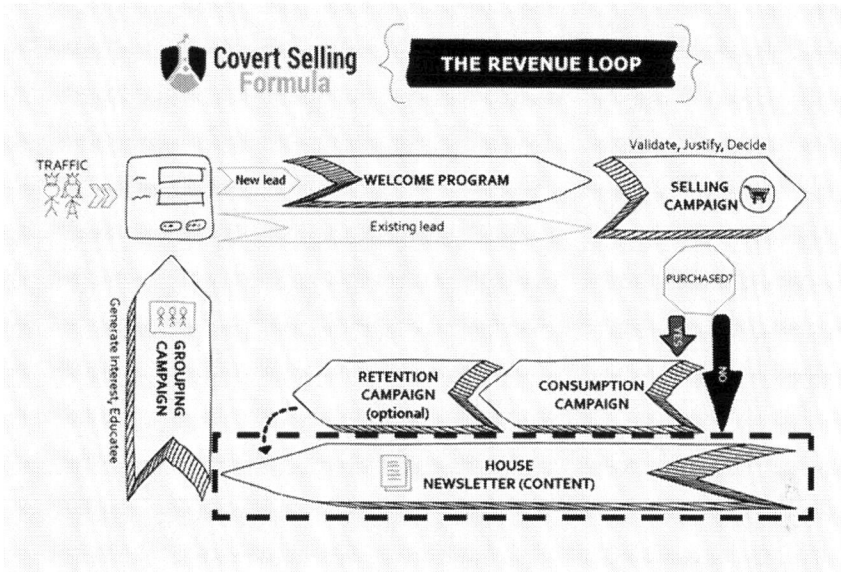

Everything defaults back to the Nurturing Phase. If you're not in the Welcome, Selling or Consumption Phases then you're in the Nurturing Phase.

What does the Nurturing Phase look like? It happens through a series of emails, the House Newsletter Campaign.

Many marketers will simply discard prospects who failed to purchase as worthless – they didn't buy, so why bother with them anymore? Practically, they would start marketing 3rd party offers to them in the hope of squeezing any dollar out of the leads or even worse, would stop marketing to them altogether.

Just because they didn't buy now – or choose to buy that specific product – doesn't mean they won't buy later. In fact, studies show how up to 81% of conversions happen after the prospect has been exposed to the offer five or more times.

The fact of the matter is that, if they are on your list, they are there because they're interested in what you're offering to some capacity, so just because they didn't purchase during your Selling Campaign, doesn't mean you should kick them to the curb.

So, what exactly is the Nurturing Phase?

The Nurturing Phase is a non-selling series of messages that

1. Informs subscribers about specific developments relating to their problem(s)

2. Provides them with value and educates them

3. Gathers information about their needs

If you're a digital marketing company for example, you can send on a weekly, bi-weekly or monthly basis:

•   Updates about changes in the Facebook algorithm (informs subscribers about specific developments)

•   Five top tips for getting free Facebook traffic, or a video on how to write the perfect blog headline (educates your subscribers)

•   A survey asking what is the number one issue with their marketing at the moment

Also, aside from keeping your prospects informed and nurturing through free, high-value information, you can also use this to monitor engagement and learn more about them. You will be able to see your open rates and specific links they are clicking on, which will allow you to group the prospects based on their engagement and interests. This will provide you with very valuable inspiration for when you run the next Grouping Campaign, as you will know what pain points are the most relevant to your audience. Once you know this, you can gear your offer to solve that problem.

Now, through any of the phases we've mentioned so far, what will begin happening is that different leads will take different actions. Some will open your emails, but not click the link inside them. Some will click a link, but not convert into a sale. Some will take advantage of one offer, while consistently ignoring other offers.

To nurture all of these leads the same way, after they start displaying stark differences in how they conduct their "digital body language", would start to disenfranchise a majority of your prospects, making them feel as though you're out of touch with their needs.

For example, keeping with the digital marketing company case, those who clicked on links relating to how to generate more traffic with Facebook would go into a specific Grouping Campaign about Facebook ads, those who clicked on how to build a better website would go into a Grouping Campaign about website optimization, etc.

In order to ensure this doesn't happen, you need to move them regularly into the Grouping Phase leads based on their engagement.

My seminar attendees often ask "What's the difference between the Consumption and the Nurturing Phases?" Essentially they are both "nurturing" phases, the key difference is that the Consumption Phase is specifically nurturing customers of a given product whereas the Nurturing Phase is nurturing everyone (non customers as well as customers who have completed the Consumption Campaign).

7. The Grouping Phase

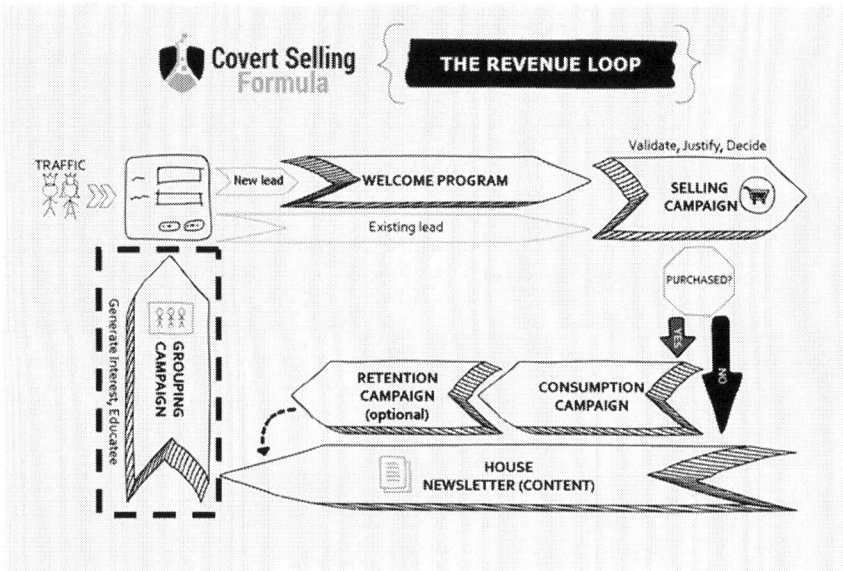

Now that you have a solid understanding of the various ways in which to welcome, convert, retain, and nurture your audience, let's now look at how to group them according to their engagement so you can provide your audience with more value and, as a result, sell more to them.

Everybody who opts-in to your list will go through a Welcome Phase, a Selling Phase and then a Nurturing Phase. Eventually, however, you may want to offer a different product to your audience or you may want to re-offer the same product to your audience (for example, if you're an accountant you may want to offer tax filing services before the end of each accounting year).

Let's say you are a coach who teaches people to live a debt-free life. In order to get people to opt into your list, you create a free webinar (the Lead Magnet). In order for people to see the webinar they have to provide their email (they opt in to your mailing list). You know that everyone who signed up for the webinar is interested in living a debt-free life.

Say 1,000 people opt-in to your Lead Magnet. They go through your Welcome Campaign and your Selling Campaign.

Let's say 30% of your list purchased during the Selling Campaign and the other 70% did not.

This would mean that 30% (300 people) would go to your Consumption Campaign while 70% (700) went into the default Nurturing Campaign.

You also have a coaching program on how to invest in property. You produce an eBook (Lead Magnet) on the "Top 5 Ways You Can Reduce Your Estate Agent Letting Fees". A couple of months after you promoted the "How to live debt-free "coaching you run your list through a new grouping campaign this time offering the property Lead Magnet. Some people will optin and go through a Selling Campaign for your property coaching, some people will pass on the offer and go back to the Nurturing Phase. Through this approach you are providing as much value as possible to your list because you are offering your audience solutions to different problems they may have, and as a result your sales grow compare to if you just promoted the "How to live debt-free" coaching

The more you group and segment, the more you understand about your lists, and the better you can market to them on an individual level.

Grouping Based on Action

The Target Segment That Increased Revenues Per Mailing By 330%!

Even though PaperStyle's business was selling custom invitations, their emails were anything but customized. They would send out the same email to their entire email database, regardless of demographic or interest. Unsurprisingly, email open and click rates started to suffer very quickly.

By looking at customer past purchase histories and by using Google Analytics they identified a segment that they could focus on; brides and/or bride's friends.

When any of the following happened the bride or the bride's friend would receive an additional, targeted promotional offer:

- Clicks on a wedding link in any Paper Style email

- Purchases wedding or bridal shower products

> - Visits a wedding-related page on the PaperStyle.com website
>
> The results?
>
> - Open rate increased 244%
> - Click rate increased 161%
> - Revenue per mailing increased 330%!
>
> *Find out more about Paper Style's story here: http://ItsTheFollowupStupid.com/paperstyle*

Let's say you don't have a diverse array of different offers, packages, coaching, and so on. Let's say you have one product/service and that's it. You can still group based on action.

For example, you have a welcome campaign where you talk about the benefits of your product, and one email provides a case study about someone having got great results with it. You could group as follows:

1. Those that received the email, but didn't open it (the subject line wasn't compelling enough to them)

2. Those that opened the email, but didn't click to download the case study (the email contents were not compelling enough to them)

3. Those that clicked to download the case study within the email, got to the download page, but didn't complete the action, they never actually downloaded it (the contents on the page wasn't compelling enough to them)

4. Those that clicked and completed the download but didn't purchase (these are your hottest prospects)

There are four different groups right here, and you should be marketing to them differently. For example:

1. Group 1 (those who didn't open the email) should be sent the same email content but with a different, more enticing subject line. This is commonly referred to as "emailing the non openers".

2. Group 2 (opened but didn't click on the link) should be sent an email with more enticing content and also a different subject line.

3. Group 3 (opened, clicked but didn't download) should be sent an email asking them how come they didn't download the report, inviting them to download it and/or you could attach the report to the email itself instead of asking them to download it from a link. If available, you can also direct them to the same content but in a different format (for example, send them to a video instead of a PDF report - they may prefer watching a video over reading).

4. Group 4 (opened, clicked, downloaded but didn't buy) should be put in a Selling Campaign.

The rule of thumb, however, is to create as many specialized, niche groups as you can, because this will allow you to create hyper-relevant campaigns. The more segmented your automated email marketing is, the higher your conversion rates and your revenues.

461% Increase In Conversion Rates Thanks To A Simple Triggered Email...

A big challenge that retailer Moosejaw Mountaineering was facing was the loss of revenues when a prospect goes to the order form page on the website, but does not go on to fulfil the transaction (often called "cart abandonment").

Moosejaw set up triggered emails to be sent out when these instances occur so as to capture lost sales.

"In one particular test, we saw users with 125% higher open rates, 168% higher click rates, and our conversion rate was up a whopping 461%, showing us that engaged users who buy into our brand, even a little bit, can provide a huge boost to our bottom line" says Eoin Comerford, SVP of Marketing & Technology.

Find out more about Moosejaw's story here:
http://ItsTheFollowupStupid.com/moosejaw

SECTION 4

FROM INSIGHT TO IMPLEMENTATION

1. How Much Does It Really Cost?

The True Cost of Marketing Automation

Automated email follow up can seem expensive, but expensive compared to what? Compared to missing out in sales? Compared to working so hard that you miss seeing your kids and grandkids grow up? Compared to not having a marketing strategy that you can sell as part of your company to potential investors? How much can a stable marketing strategy add to your company valuation? How about the cost of having to hire, train and manage staff?

Eventually, compare that small investment in marketing automation to the increase in sales, the increase in company value, and savings on payroll... Marketing automation becomes a negative cost. That's right – a **negative cost**. You increase your revenue and reduce costs at the same time. And as a bonus, chances are you will have more free time! Can you afford NOT to invest in marketing automation?

From $200,000 to $600,000 In Revenue In One Year Thanks To Automated Nurturing

Salon Success Strategies is a marketing agency in California, USA that caters to salons and spas. The founder, Heather Lemere, grew sick and tired of 16+ hour workdays at her day job so decided to quit and start Salon Success Strategies in 2009.

In its first years of operation, Heather had significant trouble qualifying those leads and turning them into customers. She made the most of automated email follow up by setting up tailored marketing campaigns that allowed not only for lead nurturing but also increased the quality of the lead as he progressed through the campaigns. Heather also used lead scoring to focus efforts on the hottest, most conversion-ready leads.

The results?

- Expenses were reduced by 30%
- Subscriptions increased 150%
- Revenue grew from $200,000 in 2013 to $600,000 in 2014
- Advertising spend was reduced by 40%
- And Heather now rarely works more than 8 hours a day!

Find out more about Salon Sucess Strategies' story here: http://ItsTheFollowupStupid.com/salonsuccessstrategies

140% Increase In Conversions By Sending Emails On "Special" Dates...

Several years ago, the world's leading online fabric store, Fabric. com, were sending out their marketing emails in-house and sending the same message to all their database of contacts.

With no customization or segmentation involved, Fabric.com realized that not taking into account individual buyer purchasing behaviors was causing them to lose their competitive edge.

Fabric.com decided to use marketing automation to send emails based on specific dates, including:

- "Happy Anniversary" emails

- "Happy Birthday" emails
- "We Miss You" emails for customers who haven't ordered in a while
- "We Want You Back" emails
- "Secret Sale" emails

The results?

- 140% increase in conversions
- 50% annual growth in revenue generated from email
- 50% reduction in people unsubscribing from the list

Find out more about Fabric.com's story here:
http://ItsTheFollowupStupid.com/fabric

2.   The PATH To Engaging Emails

How do you implement automated email follow up? You email follow ups must include a combination of these 4 types of messages. It is important that you use all four types because they all have their own purpose. The four categories that make up P.A.T.H. are:

Category 1: Promotional

Promotional emails make a specific offer to the prospect or customer, giving him the opportunity to take action, purchase a product, or contact you. It's anything that allows him to directly continue moving up through the buying cycle.

Category 2: Attachment

Attachment emails are designed to keep the prospect interested in your business and build a sense of trust. The prospect must feel you will be there for him and that you are committed to him over time, above and beyond any business he does with you. These messages build both an emotional and rational attachment to you.

Attachment emails can be made of high-value educational content but don't have to be. They can just be a three line email, like: "Hey! You know, we haven't spoken for a month. Just wanted to make sure that everything was okay. Is there anything else I can do for you?"

Category 3: Transactional

Transactional emails confirm a transaction, such as a purchase or a booking. These emails tend to have some of the highest open and click through rates they confirm a recently taken action. Yet most businesses overlook a very important "bonus" that comes with transactional emails...

Whenever a customer places an order or purchases a new item, the "feel-good" chemical dopamine is released in the reward section of his brain. This chemical is key in encouraging customers to make another purchase. Once they have made their first purchase, triggering a release of dopamine, their brains yearn for another chemical release, another dose of chemicals that will give them a sense of pleasure and satisfaction. So why not include upsells in your transactional emails? You'll be surprised by the conversion rates.

Category 4: Highlights

These are time-specific messages, for example seasons' greetings around Christmas, New Year, Valentine's Day, etc. You may talk about recent client success stories, the opening of a new office, or even the launch of a new product. Highlights are timely and generate a sense of excitement in your list that goes above and beyond the products you sell. It shows them you're a real person, a real business with things going on and your prospects want to know about it. Try it!

Not sure where to start? Templates for all of these are provided in the CovertSellingFormula.com

3. Campaign Management And Optimization

How do you get the most out of your automated email follow up? Chances are your automated follow up won't be perfect at the outset, so most of your results will come from ongoing management and optimization of the marketing automation. The 80/20 rule applies here as well; in this case 80% of your results will come from 20% of your efforts. And the campaign management and optimization is exactly this 20% worth of effort that will generate 80% of the results!

Ask yourself: What can I optimize? What aspects of marketing automation lead to the most ROI? What contributes to that 4,000% ROI that people are getting from email marketing?

What do we mean by optimization? It's simply the process of A/B testing (or split testing) different elements of your automated follow up to see which one yields the best results. For example you can test 3 different subject lines and see which one yields the highest open rate.

Here are some things you can optimize for:

- Email subject line

- Email format (plain text, plain HTML, graphical mailer)

- Email copy (its contents)

- Call to action (CTA)

- What time of the day the email is being sent

- What day of the week the email is being sent

- Segments the email is being sent to

Once you start having the data you can start optimizing on the **first level** - open rates and click-through rates. Once first level optimization is complete, you can start **second level** optimization - which is optimizing for revenues instead of open or click through rates.

780% ROI Generated Thanks To Email Testing And Optimisation

The RSPCA Charity relies heavily on its supporters for funding, hence striking the balance between soliciting donations and maintaining subscriber engagement is crucial.

One of the ways the RSPCA are using to ensure that they are striking this balance is to run A/B tests in their email campaigns.

For example to test open rates, the RSPCA carried out a subject line test. They used the two main gender segments to do this; the male segment received the subject line: "Valentine's Cards and Gifts Delivered from just £5!", and the female segment received the subject line "Valentine's Cards delivered from just £5!"

The results?

- 45% increase in open rates

- The Valentine's promotion alone added an extra 47% in revenue for the month!

Find out more about the RSPCA's story here:
http://ItsTheFollowupStupid.com/rspca

Within a very short time, you'll be able to determine which aspects of your automated follow up generate the most sales and the most leads for your sales team (if you have one). From that point on keep optimizing and watch your sales grow!

4. How Do I Measure The Success Of My Marketing Automation?

Step 1

Look at your open rates, click-through rates, unsubscribe rates, spam rates, and email bounces.

If you are investing in marketing automation do you know how much it's making you in return? Many business owners know how much they're investing but they don't know how much it's making back, so how do you measure this?

The first thing to do is to look at your **open rates** (usually measured in percentage of total emails sent). For example, if you sent 10,000 emails and the open rate is 10% that means 1,000 people opened your email. A word of caution, due to how open rates are tracked from a technical standpoint, open rates are generally an under-estimate of the actual open rate. In the example above, if your open rate is 10% chances are slightly more than 1,000 people have actually opened your email. The open rate answers the question: "How good of a job is the subject line doing in getting people to open the email?"

The second thing to do is to look at your **click through rates**. This is the percentage of people who clicked on any link within your email. Unlike open rates, click through rates (CTR) are an accurate representation of how many people completed the action (clicked on the email in this case). The CTR answers the question: "How good of a job are the email content, design and calls to action doing in getting people to click on the link in the email?"

Another factor that is extremely important is how many people have clicked on a <u>specific</u> link within the email. For example, if people are clicking on the "contact us" link, those recipients want to communicate with you in relation to something in the email. Users who click on the "Contact Us" link are perfect candidates to add to a Selling Campaign or at the very least to a Nurturing Campaign (if they are not already there). I recommend you invite these prospects to contact you through live chat, a "Reply To" email, or social media. On the other hand, people clicking on the "Who We Are" or "About Us" links in an email are still unsure about who you are and what you can do for them. They are not ready to buy and should be inserted in a Welcome Campaign (if not already in there).

My students and seminar attendees often ask me: "What's a good open rate?", "What's a good click through rate?" There's no good or bad open rate/CTR. Depending on your industry, where the list comes from, the type of content, time of the year, how often you email the list and other factors, a 20% open rate could be excellent or terrible and the same applies to click through rates. However, after looking at a few key factors in your business I can very quickly tell you what is a good or bad open/click through rate.

Next, look at **unsubscribe rates**. You need to include an "Unsubscribe" link at the bottom of every email you send. An "Unsubscribe" link allows people to either unsubscribe from all your email communications or just from specific types of communications through a preference centre. For example someone may not want to receive your weekly newsletter but may be interested in receiving special offers.

Look at how many people are unsubscribing as a percentage of emails sent. It's normal to have a certain number of people unsubscribe from your marketing communications every time you send out an email. Don't look at absolute numbers, look at percentages instead. 100 people unsubscribing out of a 500,000 list can be normal whereas 100 people unsubscribing out of a 500 list indicates an issue. A sudden surge in the unsubscribe rate may be a symptom that people don't like the content, that they have negative feelings toward your brand because of something that happened in the world, or simply that you're mailing them too often.

Is Your Unsubscribe Rate Too High?

I often get asked, "Is my unsubscribe rate too high?", "What is a 'good' unsubscribe rate?" Just like open and click through rates there is no overall benchmark on what is a good unsubscribe rates. There are a lot of sources who will tell you "0.1% is high, low etc". The truth is that just like open and click through rates, there is no 'good' numbers. It depends on your industry, product, mailing frequency, list source etc. Just like for opens and click through rates, after looking at those factors in your specific business I can very quickly tell you what is good or bad.

Is People Unsubscribing From Your List A Good Thing?

Yes, as long as it's within a reasonable range, people leaving your list is a good thing because you want to keep within your sphere of influence only people who want to hear from you. Naturally, there will be a small portion of people who were interested in your content but over time have become uninterested.

Finally, look at **spam (or complaint) rates**. How many people have reported your email as spam? This has nothing to do with whether they opted in for your lead magnet. Obviously, if you are emailing people who never opted in chances are your spam rates will be very high. It just means they <u>think</u> your email was spam. Refer back to the true definition of spam given earlier in this book. Avoiding spamming your list is not just about having the legal permission to email the subscribers but most importantly it's about sending emails that are relevant, timely, and valuable to the reader. Clicking on the spam button is a way for users to tell you that they're not connecting with your emails. High spam complaints indicate something is wrong with the email content, frequency, format or something else.

Step 2

Knowing Who Your Customer Is: Open Reach, Click Reach, Cohort Analysis, and the 80/20 Rule

What Does "Open Reach" Mean?

Open Reach allows you to determine how many total people you've reached <u>at least once</u> in a given period of time. Understand this concept and your approach to business will change forever.

Imagine you send an email the first week and the open rate is 20%. You send a second mailing the following week and also get a 20% open rate. We do this a third week and, again, the open rate 20%. What the open rate doesn't tell us is whether it's the same group of 20% of people who are opening email one, two, and three or is it a different group of people every time. If it is a different group each time, in the first case we reached 20% of the database onlyand by the third case we reached 60% of it. Clearly it's an extreme example but you get the gist. The reality is that in every list there will be a core group of people who open every single one of our emails (the hyper-responders) and a group who open only a few of your emails.

Open Reach focuses on how many people have opened at least one of your emails. It answers the question: "How many different people is my email marketing reaching out to?" What's the difference between Open Rate and Open Reach? The open rate is a <u>snapshot</u> in time of how many people opened a specific email of yours whereas Open Reach measures <u>over time</u> how many people are being exposed to your marketing, regardless of which email(s) they opened.

Similar to Open Reach, Click Reach tells you how many people have clicked on at least one your links over a given period of time. It tracks how many different people have expressed an interest in engaging with your brand over the selected period and the same distinctions apply.

Step 3

Correlating Marketing Automation with Revenue Data

Step 3 is the step that most businesses get wrong. Why? Because they stop their analysis at open, click through, unsubscribe and spam complain rates. But as a business, would you rather have higher open rates or higher sales? Therefore, when measuring the success of your automated follow up it's crucial that the data is correlated to sales. What emails generate the most sales or leads? What campaigns get most people to call up the office? You need to cross reference the subscriber's behaviour with your revenue data.

Predictive Email Marketing

As an example, let's say you find that people who have opened five or more of your emails in the last 30 days have a 90% chance of becoming customers. As soon as a lead has opened five or more emails, assign the lead a high-nurture status. This may mean sending the lead to a different automated marketing campaign or asking a salesperson to take a more personalized approach.

This avoids wasting time and effort on groups of people who are not ready to buy or who don't have the means. Now your sales team can invest their time only with leads that are highly likely to buy. Likewise, if every time you send an email to a specific person he makes a purchase, ensuring that a sale happens is easy. All you have to do to increase your revenue is email that person more often. In mine and my clients' businesses, we found that every email list has a group of "serial buyers"; people who will buy every single product you sell. Therefore, why not email that group of people more and increase your sales? By predicting how people are likely to behave, growing sales becomes easy!

RFM

Finally, another type of analysis that's extremely important to consider is RFM analysis.

'Recency' tells you how recently someone has purchased a product. For example, it's the list of people who purchased from you in the last 30 days. Because they've recently engaged and bought from you, chances are these customers are more likely to buy from you again sooner rather than later. Build a segment out of these subscribers and run them through a different Selling Campaign, for example.

'Frequency' is the answer to these questions: How frequently do these customers buy? Who are the people placing five or more transactions with you every year? Who are your best repeat buyers? These people are also more likely to buy from you again (in fact, they may be already buying more from your competitors). Putting them into a Selling Campaign would give them the opportunity to do more business with you, and who wouldn't want that?

'Money' helps you define your highest spenders. It shows you who buys your most expensive products. These subscribers are to be put in a high end Selling Campaign or can be followed up with on the phone, if possible.

Looking at your database and the three dimensions (Recency, Frequency, and Money) helps you understand who your customers are and where you should focus your marketing dollars. Best of all, using some of the best marketing automation tools available today I have helped many businesses automate this and the results have been nothing short of extraordinary!

How Meny Boosted Revenue By $1 Million Thanks To An Automated Sales Funnel!

PTEX is a marketing agency in Tennessee, USA specializing in everything from branding to websites to call centers. Its founder Meny Hoffman was concerned that the agency was flourishing but customer experience was slipping as it grew. Further, there was no concreted process in place for nurturing leads through the sales cycle.

PTEX mapped out a precise funnel within Infusionsoft including a welcome program, a selling campaign and direct mail packages sent out at every stage of the sales and retention process. This allowed Meny and his team to keep in touch with their prospect and customers without devoting significant manpower or resources to marketing.

The results?

- Reduced advertising spending by approx. 24%
- Grew the customer base by 15%
- Boosted annual revenue by over $1 million

Find out more about PTEX's story here:
http://ItsTheFollowupStupid.com/ptex

5.   Should I Insource or Outsource?

Anyone with an internet connection can send an email – even children use email for school assignments. However, sending marketing emails is very different from sending personal, one to one emails. Many businesses that do decide to follow-up with their clients through email are often disappointed with the results, and they wonder why.

This is because businesses lack experts with a solid understanding of all aspects of marketing on their team. Why? It's most often due to cost but, I've said it once and I'll say it again; if you think hiring a professional is expensive, wait until you hire an amateur! Just like when visiting a specialist doctor for example, always make sure you're working with the top professionals in the field.

There are advantages to both developing your email follow up in-house (insourcing) and outsourcing. The main thing to consider is "What is your H.A.B.U.?" "What is the Highest And Best Use of your time?" It makes more sense to outsource if you don't possess the knowledge, tools or time to design, write, implement and optimize professional email campaigns. However, if you have in-house experts who specialize in email marketing, it makes more sense to insource (even though occasionally I work with large companies with dedicated email marketing teams who prefer to outsource still).

Email marketing is a highly specialized discipline. As a great copywriter is not necessarily a great graphic designer and a great graphic designer not necessarily a great campaign manager, email marketing typically requires seven different disciplines to be successful.

What Are The Seven Disciplines?

1) **Campaign strategist** - The campaign strategist(s) will decide what message to send to what segment, with what offer, when and in what format

2) **Copywriter** - The copywriter(s) will write the actual content of the emails including the Calls To Action (CTA)

3) **Graphic designer** - The graphic designer(s) will design the graphical layout of the mailers including images, colours, fonts, etc.

4) **Web programmer (or HTML coder)** - The web programmer will convert the design that the graphic designer produced into HTML code that can be sent to the email list

5) **Email Tester and Deliverability Expert** - The email tester/deliverability expert will ensure the email doesn't get caught in the users' spam folder and will ensure that it's delivered to the inbox

6) **Campaign Manager** – The campaign manager will make sure the campaign is delivered under the best circumstances to ensure maximum results. This will include, for example, email platforms being used, send speed, any blacklists or blocks that may be encountered on the way, etc

7) **Data Analyst** - The data analyst will analyze the campaign data and provide a campaign report including KPIs such as open rate, click through rate and also revenues, Open Reach and Click Reach, etc

If you have these resources in-house or can hire them, insourcing would be the way to go. If, on the other hand, your business is not yet at the level where it would be cost-efficient for you to hire seven people for your email marketing, working with an external team of experts and outsourcing your email marketing is probably the better choice. This means hiring a third party who has experience and expertise in the seven disciplines. This third party would be able to provide you with the expertise provided by the seven specialists at a fraction of the cost to hire a team of seven.

For example, hiring a third party or outsourcing partner allows you to avoid Mistake No. 5 (lack of strategy). Staff departures and turnover can lead to serious problems. Therefore, having an external entity who demonstrates continuity on strategy, has a vision, and has the stability to provide you with a consistent marketing message will ensure you create branding that helps you stand out in front of your audience.

My private clients, for example, have access to best practices acquired over years of deploying campaigns for tens, if not hundreds, of other clients at a fraction of the cost of what it would cost to hire an in-house team of email specialists. Is dealing with email copy, the email deliverability, and coding the highest and best use of your time? If the highest and best use of your time lies elsewhere, you're better off outsourcing.

85% Conversion Rate And 37 Extra Holidays Thanks To Marketing Automation!

Dr. Burleson owns an orthodontic practice in Missouri, USA and runs his business around marketing automation. "Infusionsoft is our sales force. It's unbelievable how it automates the sales process and follow-up", says Dr Burleson.

Leads come in from various channels such as Facebook, PPC and direct mail and thanks to an automated email follow up sequence 85% of leads convert into patients compared to a national average of 50%. Of those who don't convert initially, 20% do during a nurturing campaign.

But the automation doesn't stop there. Thanks to a consumption campaign, 60% of patients refer new patients, up from just 28% before marketing automation was implemented.

The results?

- Revenues grew 180%
- Acquisition cost was reduced by 56%
- Dr Burleson went from 5 vacation days to 42!

Find out more about Dr. Burleson's story here:
http://ItsTheFollowupStupid.com/burlesonorthodontics

6. F. A. Q.

How often should I mail my prospects and my clients?

This is a very common question. You need to mail your prospects and clients with the frequency that's appropriate to the <u>specific</u> market and the <u>specific</u> subscriber. Clients in some markets like to receive email two or three times a day. Stock traders and other professionals in the financial market, for instance, work in fields that are constantly changing throughout the day. Therefore are used to receiving information in real time and may wish to receive morning, afternoon, and evening emails. In contrast, people in industries that don't move so fast, like the medical and legal industries, may be accustomed to receiving emails once a week or once a month. Regardless of the market, some subscribers prefer to receive small, daily updates about topics they're passionate about whereas others may prefer to receive a longer digest on a weekly basis.

How do you work out the mailing frequency then? Start off with your intuition - if you where in your prospect's shoes how often would you want to receive emails? Then test different mailing frequencies (daily, bi-weekly, weekly, monthly, etc) and look at open rates, click through rates and sales where possible to figure out the optimal mailing frequency.

When is the best time to send an email? What is the best day of the week?

The best time to send an email depends on the purpose of the email and the offer being promoted. Most people read commercial emails in the afternoon, between 3:00PM and 5:00PM. By this time, they have had the chance to look through their morning emails and take care of day-to-day tasks and are now experiencing afternoon dead-time.

If you're offering something that requires human interaction and requires a prospect to contact a member of your sales team, send your email between 5:00AM and 8:00AM. This will give your sales team the whole day to follow up with prospects. On the other hand, if you're offering a product that users can purchase without human interaction (ecommerce or an online eBook), the afternoon is better because people have more free time in which to place an order.

In terms of the right day to send, this also depends on the content and offer. For free content that users can consume in a few minutes, weekends are ideal because people have more time and are willing to consume light content. If, however, you're asking people to make a purchasing decision Tuesday to Thursday are typically best. Those are the days when people are in a work mindset and are often more willing to make important decisions. Mondays are far from ideal, as people are responding to events that happened over the weekend. Fridays are equally ineffective, as people are already in a weekend-mindset.

Is this a one-size-fits-all rule? No. This is what I found works best for most markets and products but perform your own testing. Getting different conclusions? Let me know at t@dvfx.com!

What should you use in the "From" field?

This is an important point that is often overlooked, yet it's so simple! I recommend using a mix of "from" names in your automated email follow up. This creates a more human connection and keeps the content fresh. The last thing you want is for your customers and clients to feel like they are engaging with a cold, robotic business. Using the name of real people within your company in your "From" field is a great way to give the email a feeling of authenticity and sincerity.

"People buy from people, not from brands"

Tiz Gambacorta

What about system generated emails like transactional emails for example? In this case it's OK to use a system generated name, a company name, or a department name.

Remember the four types of PATH emails? Promotion, Attachment, Transactional, and Highlights. As a general rule of thumb, I recommend using people's names for Promotional and Attachment emails. For Transactional and Highlight emails you can use your company name or website.

Alternating between different "from" names allows people to associate different individuals within your business to different types of communication. For example, one of my private clients is a large IT solutions provider who offers eight different solutions across eight different divisions. Each division has a product champion and the emails from each division come from the respective product champion. General announcements come from the company CEO whereas transactional emails come from the division name.

My open rates are very low, what can I do?

This can be due to a number of factors, including:

- Your email sending infrastructure - How good is your email platform at getting the emails delivered? It doesn't matter how good your messages are or how good your list is if your emails are not getting delivered to the users in the first place. I advise my clients on a number of checks to be performed (and a number of elements to be fixed, potentially) on your email platform to ensure your emails are getting delivered

- Your subject lines - How engaging are they for the subscriber? Short subject lines tend to perform the best. Stick to subject lines of eight words or less. The sole purpose of the subject line is to get the prospect or customer to open the email. Therefore, subject lines shouldn't summarize content but should offer just enough information to inspire curiosity and encourage users to open the email. For more information on how to write great subject lines, visit www.EmailExploder.com

- Your relationship with the list - How good is your relationship with your subscribers? Have you sent them a Welcome Campaign? Have you been nurturing them over time with a Nurture Campaign? For done for you campaigns (including Welcome Campaigns, Selling Campaigns, Nurturing Campaigns, etc), visit www.CovertSellingFormula.com

SECTION 5

MAKING THE WIZARDRY FOOLPROOF

1.   7-Point Landing Page Checklist

This landing page generated thousands of leads, each for less than $1.20...

What Is a Landing page?

We've talked a lot about how to create effective email campaigns, receive great open rates, and boost your conversions, but none of that means anything if you don't have leads in your list to begin with. This is where a landing page comes in.

A landing page is a webpage featuring a simple offer and is designed to provide a visitor with something valuable in exchange for (at the very least) their email address.

This valuable asset is known as a 'lead magnet'. Regardless of your niche or industry, you'll likely be able to offer some kind of digital lead magnet. It could be a case study, access to a free webinar, a white paper, an eBook, a coupon for X% off, a download/free trial of a software, a quiz/survey… the list goes on. In some cases (for example, if you're selling consumable products) you may be able to provide physical lead magnets, like a free sample or something that complements your offer. For instance, if you're offering business card printing, your lead magnet could be a business card holder.

Does the lead magnet need to expensive or limited edition? No, it just needs to have value **for the visitor at that point in time.**

When should you use a landing page? In addition to encouraging people to sign up for your email list to start with, you can also use a landing page at the beginning of the Grouping Phase. This will allow your existing subscribers to "raise their hands" to enter a new Selling Campaign for a specific offer.

Here is my personal 7-step checklist to create a high-conversion landing page.

1 Make a SINGLE, Huge Promise

One of the biggest mistakes marketers make when creating landing pages is to offer two or three (or more) benefits on the page. This confuses visitors and reduces the chance that they'll take action. Instead, promise one huge thing, and one thing alone. Whether you're offering a course or a 12-page report, find that one BIG benefit of your lead magnet that has the "wow factor." This is your lead magnet and should be the only benefit you offer in the landing page headline.

For example, if you have a case study that teaches dentists how to gain patients using online marketing and there's a specific Facebook ad mentioned in the case study, use that as your selling point. A headline for such an offer could be "Enter Your Email to Learn How to Double Your New Patient Count in the Next 4 Weeks with This Facebook Ad." It shouldn't say "And also build loyal, returning patients, get referrals... etc" because you'll draw attention away from the "one thing" that is attracting your leads.

2. Highlight the End Result

Let's say you have a guide called "The Dentists' Guide to Internet Marketing," which helps dentists gain more patients using online marketing tactics. This satisfies the specificity condition (dentists) and describes what the dentists want: more patients walking through the door. That's the end goal. The dentist isn't excited about learning online marketing and most likely isn't interested in acquiring such a skill. Mastering internet marketing is a means to an end (acquiring more patients).

Using a headline like "Click Here to Get the Dentist's Guide to Internet Marketing" won't perform particularly well because it doesn't appeal to the prospect's aims and desires. As the saying goes, "Sell the sizzle, not the sausage."

Let's say that, throughout your guide, you have three ways dentists can use to grow their email list and, as a result, their patient base – Facebook, Google Adwords, and search engine optimization (SEO).

You should create a landing page for each one.

- "Click Here to Find Out How to Gain 10 New Patients in the Next 7 Days Using Facebook"

- "Enter Your Email to Find Out How to Bury Your Competition with Just ONE Google Ad"

- "Fill Out the Form Below and Find Out How to Have Your Phone Ringing Off the Hook by Using These Simple, Free Online Tactics for Your Website"

3. Provide a Laser-Focused Solution

On your landing page, whereas you may wish to conceal how users will achieve the end result, you cannot be vague about the benefits. Visitors should be able to see the headline on the landing page and, in less than three seconds, know exactly what the specific benefits of your lead magnet are.

Lead magnets need not be complex. They should provide a specific solution to a specific problem for a specific segment of your target market. Nor do lead magnets need to be long. In fact, longer lead magnets will do more harm than good. I recommend using lead magnets that people can consume within 10 minutes. Therefore, don't offer a 200-page eBook as a lead magnet nor an hour-long video. Chances are, once the user sees the length, he'll put off reading or watching it until later – and "later" in these situations is often "never". As a subscriber is unlikely to buy anything from you until he has consumed the free content, you may end up losing a sale. The lead magnet becomes an obstacle, slowing down rather than facilitating the subscriber's progression down the funnel!

See how specific and easy to consume is this lead magnet from LeadPages?

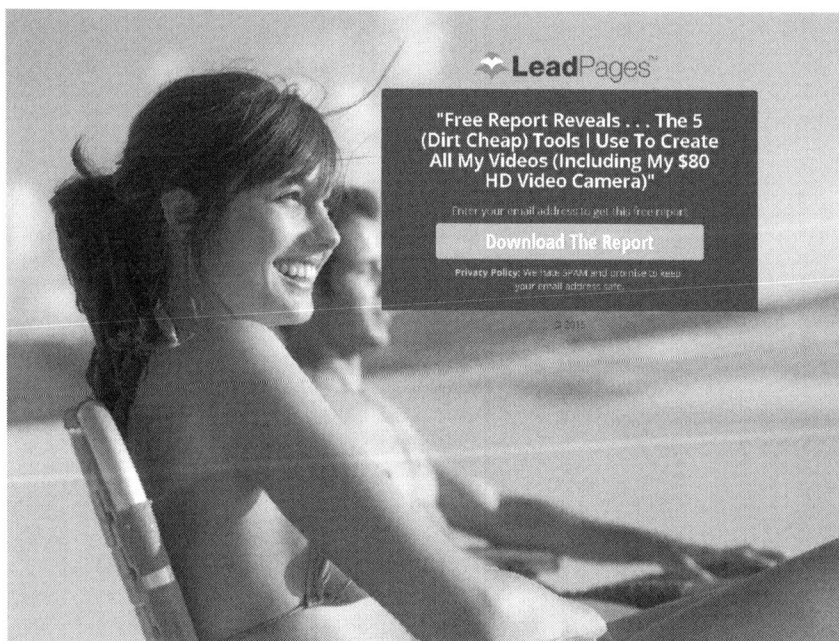

4. Create a Continuum of Belief

There are many marketers out there trying to convince prospects that what they are saying is true. They work hard to persuade a prospect they can provide him with the solution to his problems. They think the primary reason they fail to move forward with the purchase is you – the marketer or sales person. This not the case!

The main reason they don't move forward is the prospect <u>himself</u>. Prospects need to believe that, with your help, they CAN solve their problems. In fact, good marketers will never try to convince anybody of anything. They just move the prospect along a "continuum of belief," toward the solution he wants.

Imagine, for example, a 25-year-old young man, skinny and pale, who spends most of his time inside playing computer games like World of Warcraft. He doesn't have many friends and, although he has a decent job, he never gets invited anywhere.

This person decides he want to step out of his shell and change his life, starting with his physical body. No more sitting inside all day – he'll go to the gym, build up his muscle, and get the body he has always wanted. Heck, maybe he'll even find a girlfriend and some new friends in the process.

Now, let's say that you have a muscle-building supplement and an at-home exercise coaching routine that people can access via online streaming. The guy in this story already wants what you're offering – he wants to get fit and build muscle, exactly what your product promises. The biggest hurdle for your prospect at this point isn't whether or not he believes you – it's whether he can believe in himself.

Think of it this way: every day this prospect wakes up, looks in the mirror, looks at his body, and imagines what his body could be like. When presented with reality, this ideal seems impossible. Perhaps he tried other products or workout routines but didn't stick with them, becoming discouraged. He's stuck in a loop of wanting to improve his life but not being able to actually imagine himself doing so.

Your job isn't to convince this prospect that he should trust you. Your job is to lead him down that "continuum of belief", illustrating and crafting a future reality that could be his if he purchases your product. You're trying to convince this prospect to believe in himself, not to believe in you.

How do you do this? You can help him imagine how different his life could be compared to now. You can demonstrate that the difference between your offer and the ones that didn't work is that you care about him, that you care whether he reaches his goals, and you will hold him accountable through the online streaming video workouts.

What type of lead magnet would suitable here? One option could be a five-day, 10-minute-per-day routine and an eating schedule anybody can do from home, guaranteed to help with muscle building and gaining mass.

See? The lead magnet is something he can implement right now, today. However, if he REALLY wants results, he'll eventually end up going "all in," purchasing the muscle building supplement and online coaching.

The point is that the lead magnet allows him to do something simple and effective – something that is valuable to him – right this second and start seeing results. If he can do this 10-minute workout, he can handle your coaching program.

5. Construct High Perceived Value

The lead magnet you offer on your landing page will be free, but that doesn't mean it should LOOK free. Everything about it should appear expensive – great graphics and professional imagery to establish monetary value in the eyes of the visitor. Remember, people don't buy products online, they buy <u>images</u> of products.

6. Deliver High Value

When you are capturing leads through your landing page, you're essentially playing a "long-game" strategy. If you create a lot of perceived value but, when prospects download the offer, the value simply isn't there, you'll lose trust and sabotage your future marketing attempts. No matter what, make sure the value of your lead magnet is not only perceived, it must also be a reality. "Sell the sizzle, not the sausage" in your landing page, but make sure there is a sausage once the prospect opts in!

7. Fast and Furious

To obtain your lead magnet, prospects should be able to gain access and consume the lead magnet offer quickly, in as few steps as possible. Ideally, they should be able to enter their email to immediately gain access. The entire process should take less than a couple of minutes.

Furthermore, the lead magnet itself should be easy to consume. It should be short, sweet, and valuable, allowing the consumer to gobble down the information and find value quickly. Think in terms of 10 pages and 10 minutes.

2.   Need To Increase Traffic To Your Website?

All the above advice is useless if you have a lack of traffic coming to your website to begin with. However, there is some good news: there are billions of users online, constantly seeking out new, interesting, and useful information. All you need to do is direct them to your site.

There are many methods you can use but not all are easy, cost-efficient, and reliable. In addition, changes to Google and Facebook algorithms mean that the best tactics are always changing. To be successful, you need to stay up-to-date with current strategies.

There's one way to do this that will cost you nothing. Sign up at http://ItsTheFollowupStupid.com/traffic and you'll gain free, current advice for gaining traffic.

3. 70 Online List-Building Strategies and Platforms

1. Affinity Marketing – partnering with another company to create a symbiotic relationship that will help generate leads for both of you. This strategy has been responsible for over six figures worth of income across my businesses in the last four years.

2. Blogs – create your own blog to engage an audience of people who are looking for your solution

3. Bookalogs

4. E-Catalogues

5. Contests and Sweepstakes

6. Video Demonstrations

7. eBay

8. Line Extensions

9. Link Building

10. Mini Media

11. Special Offers

12. Paid Search

13. Podcasting

14. Premiums and Gifts

15. Promotions

16. Live Chat – 24/7 Salespeople Available for Troubleshooting

17. Search Engine Optimization

18. Live Online Seminars

19. Sponsorship – sponsor specific blogs, YouTube channels, or websites

20. Testimonials on Your Website

21. Viral Marketing

22. Clear and Concise Website

23. Training Video Series

24. Free Trials

25. Webinars

26. eBooks

27. White Papers

28. Set of Bonus Tips in Marketing Campaigns or Emails

29. Interview with an Expert on a Relevant Topic

30. Google AdWords

31. LinkedIn Ads

32. YouTube Videos

33. Facebook Fan Pages

34. Facebook Ads

35. Twitter

36. Paid Bloggers Writing About Your Business

37. E-zines

38. Points System – points card or customer loyalty program

39. Referral Systems

40. Networking

41. Website/E-Commerce

42. Special Events and Promotions

43. Advertorials and News Stories

44. Brochures and Corporate Literature

45. Newsletters

46. Competitors' Resources

47. Online Exhibitions and Trade Shows

48. CrunchBase – an online list generating site where can find your demographic

49. Gated Videos – the site www.wistia.com offers Wistia's Turnstile, allowing you to add opt-in forms to videos

50. Downloadable Posts in Exchange for Email Addresses

51. CTA on Your "About Us" Page

52. Evergreen Content

53. Followerwonk – this website enables you to identify fruitful leads

54. Promote Your Tweets and Link to a Landing Page

55. Articles on LinkedIn

56. Twitter Cards

57. Quora – you can answer users' queries and link back to your site or landing page

58. Slideshare – link to your landing page in presentations, descriptions, and your profile

59. Google+ Communities

60. GetApp – a site where you can pay for exposure across a portfolio of websites

61. Your Signature – add a link to your email signature that directs prospects to your landing page

62. AdRoll – allows you to "follow" people who have been to your website, over time encouraging them to come back and make a purchase

63. Pop-Ups

64. Launch-Bit – find and sponsor email newsletters that share your target audience. This will allow you to advertise your marketing campaigns and target more leads

65. Social Hubs – embed a social hub directly on your site and insert CTAs to collect leads from your social content

66. Data.com – focuses on streamlining your lead generation

67. Drip – implements pop-up technology to attract interested leads and adds them to your marketing system

68. Temper.io – measures how customers and prospects feel about your business

69. Online Quizzes – create fully customizable quizzes with Interact at www.tryinteract.com

70. Monitor Twitter Hashtags – an effective way to remain socially relevant, find out what your customers are saying about your brand, and connect with users

4. Become A Celebrity In Your Marketplace

Everything we've discussed so far in this book will work, but only if you use humanity in your marketing. The only way to humanize your marketing efforts is to sell yourself more than you sell your products/ services because, like it or not, you are intrinsically linked. To do this, you need a personality that persists throughout your marketing efforts and that positions your business as an authority. You have two options here. The first is to create a "persona" who stands for your brand and your offerings. This persona can be based around one of the company's founders, but it doesn't have to be. The second option is to build a "mascot" around your business and offerings, someone to whom people can relate.

Let's consider Progressive Insurance as an example. Progressive, by all accounts, is a big box brand, but it has no real persona. Instead, they created their unique mascot Flo – a savvy insurance clerk/concierge girl – to market and build authority.

As they had no specific PERSON for their target demographic to relate to, they created one.

People buy people; they buy personality. People buy from people they know, like, and trust. Consider some of the biggest brands today with a large marketing budget – most customers relate to the person behind the brand at least as much as they relate to the brand itself. (Think Steve Jobs of Apple, Mark Zuckerberg of Facebook, and Sir Richard Branson of Virgin). Even gigantic businesses that don't need to create a singular personality still do, simply to create an association for their audience. It's one of the most effective psychological triggers available.

Because people like Flo, they like Progressive Insurance

Flo represents EVERYONE who works at Progressive Insurance. Sure, we know she's an actress, that she's not real, and that all the people working for Progressive couldn't possibly be like her. But guess what? Even knowing this, most of us are more likely to associate trust with Progressive, more than with another insurance agency without such personality association.

When a brand becomes a physical personality we like and trust the brand more because we feel like we know the brand. We've invested time in getting to know the mascot and we've invested emotions into feeling connected to that mascot's personality. We go back to the mascot over and over again like an affectionate puppy, and brands know that.

From the Aflac duck to the Geiko gecko, from Mr. Clean to the Pillsbury Doughboy and Tony the Tiger, brands have shown that we buy personality over practicality.

Who has polar bears every Christmas? Who has the Santa Claus commercials? Coca-Cola – and what does Pepsi have? Nothing. Pepsi has its logo and its insistence that its product tastes better. Even though Pepsi shows all possible practical value, it can't compete with the fact that Coke has infinitely better branding by personality association. When you're associated with Santa Claus, no one cares if you actually taste better. When your brand has cute polar bears that give consumers a warm-and-fuzzy feeling and is able to become synonymous with the holidays, consumers are going to purchase your product over the competition because of the way it makes them FEEL.

If people feel like they know you, they'll automatically trust you. It's as simple as that.

Today's greatest authors and speakers – people who command million dollar product launches, charge $5,000 per head for seminars, and whose word is taken as law – all have origin stories.

For example, take Brendon Burchard, author of the New York Times bestseller *The Millionaire Messenger* and *The Motivation Manifesto*. His entire brand, authority, writing, seminars, and lessons centre on one theme – his origin.

At age 19 on a dark Caribbean night, Brendon narrowly survived a car accident. As he was standing on the hood of his wrecked car, bleeding, he suddenly faced the concept of his mortality. He realized, in that moment between life and death, that – in the end – everyone will ask, "Did I live? Did I love? Did I matter?"

Since that night, Brendon Burchard has dedicated his existence to help millions of people transform their lives.

All Brendon Burchard's brand marketing is dependent upon his origin story. But he's not the only one to use such a concept.

Take another hugely popular contemporary – Frank Kern. He's a highly successful Internet marketer and considered by many as a guru and top-rated copywriter. His information products typically launch at $1,197 minimum and his seminar seats can go for as much as $25,000.

Yet, at every event, in every book, and in every product, he goes back to HOW he got to where he is today. He tells his origin story of how he started as a door-to-door salesman for a credit card processing company in Macon, GA. He talks about the rejection he received and the trailer he returned home to every night. He recounts that his only aspiration at that time was to upgrade his home from a single trailer to a double-wide. He explains how he borrowed some Tony Robbins tapes from his step-father and started to formulate the mindset of a successful Internet Marketer. After hiring someone to write the eBook "Teach Your Parrot to Talk," Frank was receiving an income of $3,000 a month. He carried on to find out what other pet-styled products he could sell.

Look at any marketing celebrity out there – any brand or individual worth paying for advice, services, or products – and you're going to find a centralized origin story of how they got to where they are today. You're going to find that this origin story is the CORE of everything they do; their entire image.

You Are a Superhero

Superheroes aren't real – we all know that – but we love them anyway. Why do people love superheroes though? It isn't because they have powers – that's not particularly what makes them cool or interesting.

What make superheroes (or heroes, for that matter) dynamic, interesting, popular, and relatable are two things:

- Their origin stories

- Their weaknesses and how they overcome them

A superhero without a weakness and origin story is not worth reading about.

Take Batman – he comes from an elite family, he has all the money in the world, and he possesses no actual superpowers. But when his mother and father are murdered in front of him, he vows to combat crime and serve justice in a corrupt city by learning the skills necessary for such an endeavour. Without this origin story, there is no Batman.

Now, look at Spider-Man. What makes him interesting isn't the fact that he was bitten by a radioactive spider and can now climb walls and shoot webs out of his fingers. It's that he saw his Uncle Ben die in front of him, by a thief whom he previously had the chance to capture. He learned that "with great power comes great responsibility," a mantra his character wrestles with throughout the comics.

From Brendon Burchard's life-threatening accident, which transformed him into a motivational powerhouse, to Frank Kern's lonely single-trailer existence in rural Georgia, listening quietly at night to inspirational Tony Robbins talks, hoping to one day make it big, we all have our own superhero origin story.

You don't need to have a brush with death, a grisly murder in your family, or be in extreme poverty before you can create a core origin story for your brand. In fact, I hope none of these things ever happen to you. But you DO have to have a story, even if your life doesn't seem particularly interesting.

Even if you had a great upbringing, have never been stuck for money, went to a top college, have a fantastic family, and just want to learn how to make more money marketing your current business, YOU have a fundamental core inspirational story about who you are and how you arrived where you are today.

Establishing this core story is the backbone of your brand and message. It's the fundamental glue that holds your intrinsic authority and value together.

Without a core origin story, you have no authority and no value.

How to Develop Your Core Origin Story

There are three types of superhero origin stories:

- **Trauma** – Our hero experiences some kind of personal trauma, a stress-induced growth that causes him to alter his path and gain a new realization. This trauma is life-altering and impactful. This could be a death in the family, poverty, a near-death experience, or getting fired from a job. It could even be something as basic as stress from working for years in a dead-end corporate environment or trying to open a business and failing miserably.

- **Destiny** – Our hero discovers his true talent and calling, something that was unknown to him previously. Although reluctant, the hero throws himself into his new work by assuming great responsibility before his time. In real life, we see this a lot with sports superstars, like Manny Pacquiao, a record-breaking boxer, pro-basketball player, businessman, and, most recently, politician. Born into extreme poverty, along with five siblings, to a single mother, he began to seek his destiny at the age of 16. Destiny could involve taking on a lot of responsibility at an early age – helping your parents, helping your siblings, having to provide for yourself before most other people. Maybe you put yourself through school, lifted yourself up from your bootstraps, all to achieve your destiny.

- **Sheer Chance** – This is akin to Spider-Man, who was using his power for selfish purposes until his uncle was murdered by the same street thug he let go only hours earlier. Sheer chance transformations can be a "eureka" moment – perhaps you were walking in the woods one day, evaluating your life, when you had a sudden realization that caused you to dramatically shift your focus in your life to achieve a certain goal. Maybe you were working in the same field for decades without seeing much success until, one day, out of nowhere, someone said something that completely changed the way you approached your job and, since then, you've been a success. These are all examples of "chance" transformations that lend credibility and authority to a core story.

Which One Are You?

Everyone reading this right now should be able to identify with one of the three above origin story types, at least to some extent. Even if you don't consider your life incredibly interesting, SOMETHING has happened to you that put you on the track you're on now.

Ask yourself the following questions:

- **What do I want?** – Most people have a basic understanding of what they want.

- **Why do I want it?** – This question where most people falter. Ask somebody why they want to be a life coach and they'll say, "Because I like helping people." Ask someone why they want to own a bakery and they'll say, "Because I like baking." These reasons are too general. WHY do you like helping people? WHY do you like baking? What situations happened in your life to set you on this course? This is where your origin story comes in. It's your "why." It's this aspect of your brand and your personal reasons for creating the business you should spend the most time on.

- **How am I going to get it?** – This is where you start to develop a game plan. When Brendon Burchard figured out why he wanted to tell his story, he decided to write a book and learn how to market it. When Frank Kern learned why he wanted to accomplish his goals, he figured out how to market to a little-known niche.

Write Your Own Character

Once you've answered the above questions, one of the best ways to develop your core origin story is to write about yourself as if you were creating a character. Do this by thinking in the third-person. Imagine you're a comic book creator, or a police profiler trying to figure out who is this new masked hero in town. Start by piecing together the character's life to figure out who he is and why he does what he does. Create a name for your character (perhaps a business name or brand name) and write the harrowing story of how he came to be – the series of events that culminated to create this new hero.

You need to spend time on this – be diligent. Write your story in a hundred different ways if you have to, whatever it takes to become so ingrained in your mind that it becomes your core story.

Great authoritative brands are created in this way. Your origin story is central to success – everything else comes from it: your brand name, your tagline, your mission statement, your elevator pitch.

5.   The Four Authority Archetypes

There are four primary authority archetypes. Depending on your core message, origin story, and business, you will most likely fall into one of these areas:

- **The Advocate** – You see this a lot with legal groups, lawyers on TV, financial groups, and debt consolidation companies. These are the guys that are going to fight for you, stand up for you – in a way, they'll be your "bodyguard." They're the ones that are going to take care of the little guy and stand up to bullies. An advocate will do everything he can to empower you, enabling you to take care of your problems yourself. But, if you really need it, he'll step in and take care of the issue for you.

- **The Educator** – This is a common role in communication marketing, very much a "humble teacher" role. Imagine an educator saying, "Look, I know what I'm talking about. I have the knowledge you need, but I don't need to shout it from the rooftops." Educators will not only give you news about a problem, they'll also tell you how to solve it. Journalists, reporters, and newscasters all fall into this category.

- **The Expert** – In the movie *Taken*, Liam Neeson's character says, "I have a very particular set of skills that make me a nightmare for people like you." That's how the expert is. He has a skill set that makes him a nightmare for his competition. Unlike the educator, who may possess a variety of skills, allowing him to teach in a variety of related disciplines (like how a classroom teacher teaches art, history, and social sciences, for example), the expert has a SPECIFIC skill set in which he concentrates. Most of the time, this skill set is in a very drilled-down niche. To a certain extent, everyone should try to stay as specific as possible, although many people are able to branch out into other niches over time. The expert, however, seeks only to become better at one thing.

- **The Celebrity** – The celebrity essentially defines a marketplace. Take Dr. Oz, for example. He defines the health field for millions of viewers. His face IS modern medicine. This type of authority is all-encompassing. Rush Limbaugh, for example, is the FACE of all conservative radio. When you say conservative radio, you think of Rush Limbaugh. Think how KFC changed when Colonel Sanders decided to make his face the logo for the company. At that moment, he, as a person, became inseparable from the brand. He WAS the business because he created celebrity around it. Celebrity status means that you are indistinguishable from your brand. You and your brand are one and the same.

You don't necessarily need to choose an authority archetype for yourself. Most people will naturally fall into a category. However, if you want to aim for a certain direction to fulfil a certain archetypal role, feel free to try. There's nothing wrong with that.

Remember – you're a hero and you have a story. Find that story and you'll have found your value as a marketing celebrity.

6. The Top 100 Email Subject Lines You Can Adapt

The following 100 subject lines are easily adaptable for your audience. You can replace "[your name]" with the first-name code used by your email marketing platform. For instance, in Aweber, applying {!firstname_fix} will automatically input the first name of each lead into the subject line.

Let's say John Moriarty signed up to your list. When you input your platform's first-name code, such as Aweber's {!firstname_fix}, it will look like this: Hey John, did you see this?"

Rather than taking the adaptable subject lines as they are, use them for inspiration. For instance, instead of "28 Tips for [insert your niche] You Can't Afford to Miss," you could use "3 Big Secrets Marketers Need to Know". It's different, but it uses a similar structure.

- [Your name] here with your [insert your giveaway]

- Did you download the [insert giveaway] Ok?

- 7 secrets most [insert niche] will NEVER know…

- 6 secrets of [Insert benefit your product/service provides]

- 28 tips for [insert your niche] you can't afford to miss

- 5 steps to staying sane with [insert your niche]

- 21 Ways To [Insert benefit you provide]

- The #1 mistake most [insert niche] makes

- Checklist: Are you [insert problem you solve]?

- Here's the bad news about [insert niche]

- 5 Ways To Avoid [Insert problem you solve]

- The scary truth about [insert your niche]

- [The solution you provide] "they" don't want you to know

- Are you headed for [insert problem your service solved]?

- [Insert big benefit]! 24 great ideas

- [Insert big benefit]! 84 great tips

- Details on my [insert system or problem solved] here in today's

- [prestigious thingy]

- [First name]…a quick heads up

- [First name]…got an idea to run past you

- [Your name] finally solves [insert problem or solution you solve]

- [Your Name] here with a quick question

- [Your Name] is trying to reach you

- [Your Name] wants you to join his inner circle

- The information [First name] requested

- 2 free passes for you [First name]

- Sorry [First name] – I gotta disagree…

- [First name], I need your shipping address

- [First name], where can I send you your FREE [insert freebie]

- 5 Lessons Learned From [Insert Well-Known Person In The News]

- Have you been [insert problem you solve]? Check here…

- Did you forget to [insert problem you solve]? Take this test…

- [Insert niche] Checklist: Done all 22 Things?

- Did you forget to [insert problem you solve]? Find out…

- 27 simple ways to [insert problem you solve]

- 16 shortcuts for [insert niche]

- Top 10 tips for [insert problem you solve or benefit you provide]

- 55 keys to [insert niche]

- [insert controversial thing in your niche] is dead?

- [insert product launch] closing down?

- How to [insert big benefit for customer]

- Your [insert problem you solve] is broken…

- The Story Of [Insert crazy story for email]

- My favourite [insert niche] tool

- The Ultimate [insert niche] Cheat Sheet

- [Case Study] How To [insert transformation your business provides]

- Will this [insert pain your prospects are avoiding] in 2015?

- [TONIGHT] My proven [insert your system] Revealed…

- [Last Chance] Create the [insert transformation you provide]

- [PROOF] How to [insert big benefit you provide]

- [Free Book] How to [insert name of giveaway]

- [FLASH SALE] This is how we [insert big benefit you provide]

- [Open NOW] The [insert launch] is LIVE!

- [insert product] comes down in 1 HOUR

- The Perfect [insert transformation you provide]

- [Insert big benefit] in 3 days or less?

- [Closing Tomorrow] Don't get shut out…again!

- Good News…Your [insert transformation you provide] In 3 Days

- How I get [insert benefit] in [insert short timeframe]

- [FINAL PLAYING] Emergency [insert niche] Webinar!

- [insert launch product] Only 43 Spots Left!

- [JUST RELEASED] [announce product launch]

- [FLASH SALE] Get [insert fast result] for [insert short timeframe]

- [FINALLY] Get This Proven [Insert product]

- You a [insert seemingly unattainable result you provide, for example "millionaire"]?

- The lazy person's way to [insert result or problem solved]

- Last Chance – [product launch] Closing at Midnight TONIGHT!

- [NEWS] Announcing [insert event or product launch]

- Only open if you want to [insert transformation you provide]

- [Insert product launch] is CLOSING

- Can I help [insert transformation you provide]

- [Your service] Vs. [Another way prospects can get the transformation you provide] REVEALED...

- Last Chance For [insert freebie] [FREE RESOURCE]

- Turn [Insert tangible asset] into [insert transformation you provide]

- The "Mystery Man" Behind [insert big benefit]

- "Insider" [insert Niche] Secrets "They" Don't Want You To Know...

- Arrested for [insert big benefit]?

- Ex-[insert unrelated job or profession] becomes [insert dramatic result]

- [RESULTS] My [insert niche] Case Study

- This [insert dramatic result] by [insert percentage i.e. "24%"]

- FINAL NOTICE: [insert deadline of event, freebie, or product launch]

- Only [insert specific number] left of [insert product]

- No [insert 2 disqualifiers] = [insert dramatic result] in 3 days?

- Happy Thanksgiving [or any other holiday]!

- How I exposed the TRUTH about [insert result]

- Your Deadline Is Tonight [82% Off [insert product]]

- [REVEALED] Turn [asset into result you provide]…

- Open up, it's [insert your name]

- What [insert two things that don't go fit together] can teach you about [insert your niche]

- How to [insert result] without [insert what they don't have to have, learn, be, etc. to get result]

- 27 Ways To Kill [insert result you provide and they don't want to lose]

- Tell your [insert common enemy] what you REALLY think

- The Upcoming [insert niche] Crisis

- 5 Reasons Why You Should [Insert what you want to convince them to do]

- [Insert dramatic result] while you sleep [or other passive activity]

- 10 Lazy Ways To [Insert result you provide]

- Tired of [insert negative result or problem your prospects endure]?

- Will [insert your product or service] Allow You To [insert result you provide]?

- Do you think you can [insert conventional result]? Think again!

- Why [insert Celebrity] Uses [product/service related to yours]

- Discover The [insert transformation you provide that's quick, easy, etc.]

- Top 10 Secrets To [insert result you provide your prospects]

- Why Most [Insert group of people i.e. "Alaskans" or "Accountants"] Use [Insert product/service related to yours]

- For [insert target market] who hate [insert conventional dislike]

- What every [insert target market] must know about [insert niche]

- Confidential To [Insert target market]

- 9 Strategies For [insert result you provide]

- Quick Tips For [insert big benefit for prospect]

- Soon, [insert "fear" and "doom and gloom" scenario]

- Stop [insert problem prospects want solved]

- Last chance to [insert problem your product/service solves]

- 7 Annoying [common problems your target market endures and wants solved]

- 10 jaw-dropping [insert unconventional ways to get the transformation you provide]

- How A Shocking New [insert intro to crazy story...]

- Avoid [insert problem to be solved] with this one weird trick

- You won't believe what [insert intro to crazy story]

- How [insert underdog] was able to [insert dramatic result] by 98%

- Going...going...70% off [insert product] is almost gone!

- It's all over [insert date and time]

- 12 Things You Didn't Know About [Insert benefit]

- 9 Easy [insert niche] Hacks That'll [insert benefit]

- How To Increase [Insert big benefit]

- Struggling To [insert common problem your target audience wants solved]?

- Why [insert contrarian strategy to the solution you provide] Is The Wrong Strategy

- [First name], You Might Also Like [insert product]

- 5 [insert benefit] Tips You Haven't Thought About

- Do NOT Commit These [Insert Niche] Atrocities

- Why Most [Insert target market] Are DEAD Wrong About [insert transformation]

- Want a better way to [insert transformation you provide]

- Breaking News from [insert your name or company's name]

- Breaking down the anatomy of a [insert subject related to transformation you provide]

- 6 Sure-fire methods to [insert result]

- 8 Top Tips: How to [insert result you provide]

- [Insert alternative way to get the transformation you provide] SUCKS For [insert transformation] Here's why.

- Rise Of The [insert common enemy]

- Do your [insert things your prospects do to get the result you provide] pass this test?

- A scientific way to [insert big benefit]

- [Insert amazing result]. Find out how…

- Why a 5 year old can [insert strategy your competition uses]

- Announcing 5 ways to [insert big benefit] without [pain to avoid]…

- Problem with your [insert subject pertaining to your niche]

- 5 Uncommon Ways To [Insert big benefit]

- This sells for [insert price] today – yours free

- How to [insert result]? [Free Training]

- How [insert common method or technique] can actually HURT [insert transformation you provide]

- Confessions Of A Former [insert where your prospect was *before* their transformation]

- PROOF that [insert your product or service] will [insert big benefit]

- For more subject lines and subject line construction templates, you can refer to the "C Swipe" section in the Email Exploder course (www.EmailExploder.com)

7.   The Top 100 Email Subject Lines You Can Copy

In the last chapter we provided a list of subject lines you can adapt and personalize. In this chapter, we're offering you a list of subject lines to copy/paste and still see great results. In other words, you don't need to add any personalization, such as industry, niche, or name.

However, that isn't to say you cannot adapt these as well. For example, you could turn "Just checking in" into "Just checking in [first name]". You could take "Quick question for you" and adapt it to "Can I ask you a quick question?"

The possibilities are endless. All of these subject lines are flexible, allowing you to test and see what works best!

- A valuable lesson from a subscriber…

- Just checking in

- Been a long time

- I'm back

- Quick question for you

- Hey

- When I get to the office

- When you have a few minutes

- It's been a while

- Sorry I forgot about you

- A quick message from…

- What do you think?

- Oooops!

- This is stupid

- This is a game changer…

- Breaking News…

- Everybody's waiting for you…

- Need my help?

- I hope they're not mad…

- This changes everything…

- Will 2016 be better than 2015?

- 85% sale ends today

- This is important

- Important letter to you

- Did you miss this yesterday?

- Did you see this?

- This #1 "weird trick" is worth it….

- BAD NEWS

- Bad news and good news…

- This changed me…

- If I had to start it all over again…

- Wanna pick my brain?

- I feel kinda sorry for you…

- Good news for people who love bad news…

- CONFIDENTIAL

- Why you could be in danger…

- Last Friday I was scared…

- Rough day?

- Do NOT Make This Mistake

- Don't Screw This Up

- Shhh…This Sale Is A Secret

- 3 Sales, 4 Days Left

- We cannot offer this all day…

- New shipment selling out quick, pre-order yours today

- Act now to get the last discount

- We love you. So, we're giving you…

- You didn't win, but here's 15% off instead

- How I know you

- I have a problem

- Don't do this…

- I need to ask you a question…

- Don't forget this…

- I couldn't keep this secret…

- Happy New Year! 5 WaysTo Make 2016 GREAT

- 7 Critical Things You Need To Be Successful

- [BREAKING NEWS]: New 75-page book shipped to your door

- "This made my profits rise to 109%…"

- The Peyton Manning Secret that's my BIGGEST discovery

- How to harvest wealth versus needing income

- The lie you've been told about advertising

- Dangerous stuff man, dangerous stuff…

- ~FirstName~, why didn't you do this?

- Six Sales Lessons You Can Use Today

- One of the best success parables ever crafted…

- Disturbing truth…

- 4 Reasons Why Some People Have More Money

- The SECRET to a Worry-Free Business

- Athank you to all the entrepreneurs out there…

- #1 skill to master to increase your income

- 5 Things To Do Now To Make 2014 The Best

- I've Finally Released It...

- The secret of my success...laid out for you

- Three Ways to Show Up Like No One Else

- Live The Life Most People Can't

- The secret of my success...laid out for you

- The 5 best marketing strategies...

- Keep reading or miss out big time...

- The 12 Most Lucrative Products You'll Ever Find

FINAL THOUGHTS

I hope you realize by now that there are dozens of ways you can double your business (and income) at zero cost and create your own "economy", thanks to automated email follow up.

Think about this for a minute. If you have a business and don't leverage automation, you can only increase your earnings by working longer hours or hiring more staff. If you leverage automation on the other hand, you can increase your earnings by:

- Using a Welcome Program to build a relationship with your prospects!

- Using a Selling Campaign to do all the selling for you!

- Using a Consumption Campaign to build a following of raving fans for you, your business and your brand!

- Using a newsletters and long term nurturing to keep in constant contact with your prospects so you are the first person they think about when they are ready to buy!

- Using a grouping campaign to serve and sell to your audience over and over and make the right offer at the right time to the right prospect!

- ...and many more ways!

"Never, Ever Stop Chasing Your Dreams"

When I attended that first seminar in London in June 2010, I was sceptical at first. I thought it was a scam. The truth is that I was afraid of trying something new in case I failed. But eventually I decided it was worth taking the chance. And, sure enough, I did try something new and I did fail. But, I am glad I did. I now have days where I make thousands of dollars in profit whilst travelling the world, visiting some of the most exotic locations. Had I not taken the chance, I would still be glued to a desk in my "golden handcuffs" job as a banker.

Next steps

I hope you enjoyed reading this book. As I continue to seek out new and exciting ways of leveraging automated email follow up that can help grow your business, look out for other books being released in this series.

If you would like to join my email list to receive my weekly newsletter, watch my recorded seminars and webinars, or want to find out more about the "It's The Follow Up, Stupid" live seminars, go to http://CovertSellingFormula.com.

You can also apply to join the Covert Selling Formula Coaching Program at http://CovertSellingFormula.com/coaching.

I would love to meet you in person at one of our live events, and I would love to hear your automated email follow up success story even more! Visit http://ItsTheFollowUpStupid.com/testimonials and drop us a line. Every quarter we award the best success story with a complimentary seat in our Covert Selling Formula Coaching Program.

Did you enjoy this book? If so, don't forget to leave a review here: http://amzn.com/B01CH5MM06. We may be selecting some reviewers at random with surprise gifts to say 'thank you'.

The email marketing automation revolution has just started. I hope you will join us.

TABLE OF THIRD PARTY CASE STUDIES AND SOURCES

1. Michelle Dale - Entrepreneurs Journey blog, Entrepreneurs-Journey.com

2. Joel Friedlander - Entrepreneurs Journey blog, Entrepreneurs-Journey.com

3. Bridgevine - Silverpop, Silverpop.com

4. Iron Tribe Fitness - Infusionsoft customer success stories, Infusionsoft.com

5. Dana Levy - Harvard Business Review, Hbr.org

6. Olivier Roland - Entrepreneurs Journey blog, Entrepreneurs-Journey.com

7. Milk More as an example of how follow up helped them increase conversion rates

8. Morgan Brown - Entrepreneurs Journey blog, Entrepreneurs-Journey.com

9. LV - Econsultancy blog, Econsultancy.com

10. Optibike - Infusionsoft customer success stories, Infusionsoft. com

11. Tom Menditto - Entrepreneurs Journey blog, Entrepreneurs-Journey.com

12. Select Photo-Graphics - Infusionsoft customer success stories, Infusionsoft.com

13. Minutes Matter - Infusionsoft customer success stories, Infusionsoft.com

14. Original Runner - Infusionsoft customer success stories, Infusionsoft.com

15. Joanna Penn - Entrepreneurs Journey blog, Entrepreneurs-Journey.com

16. Fran Kerr - Entrepreneurs Journey blog, Entrepreneurs-Journey. com

17. RWE - Econsultancy blog, Econsultancy.com

18. Swim Fitness - Infusionsoft customer success stories, Infusionsoft.com

19. Amazon $300m Button - User Interface Engineering blog, Uie. com

20. Paper Style - Silverpop, Silverpop.com

21. Moosejaw - Silverpop, Silverpop.com

22. Fabric.com - Silverpop, Silverpop.com

23. Salon Success Strategies - Infusionsoft customer success stories, Infusionsoft.com

24. RSPCA - Silverpop, Silverpop.com

25. PTEX - Infusionsoft customer success stories, Infusionsoft.com

26. Burleson Orthodontics - Infusionsoft customer success stories, Infusionsoft.com

16473841R00092

Printed in Great Britain
by Amazon